As Alive, So Dead
Investigating the Paranormal

the memoirs of
Mary Ann Winkowski
as told to David Powers

Graveworm Press
Cleveland, Ohio

As Alive, So Dead is a work of nonfiction. This book is based on actual experiences and events. Certain names, places, and other identifying details may have been changed, or several cases combined into one coherent narrative, to preserve the privacy of the clients.

ISBN: 1-929309-10-4
ISBN-13: 978-1-929309-10-8

20111120-CS
second edition

For my husband, Ted, and my two girls, Amber and Tara.

And with special thanks to Richard and Mary Kruzel.

Contents

Prologue

Darkness surrounded the car like a sheet; silence pressed out from the front seat and seemed to further smother us. My husband and I hadn't said more than a few words since leaving the card party at our friends' house, and for good reason. Ted watched the head-lights pierce the black road as the car carried us gently home, and I knew the time had come to tell him the truth. His eyes said as much—said they knew I was hiding something, though he also understood it was not a malicious lie. After two years of marriage, we had come to know each other's rhythms pretty well, and I had lately come to the conclusion that, if this was the man I had chosen to spend the rest of my life with, then he had the right to know the one thing about me that, however unseen, was to become the guid-ing force of my life.

"Hon," I stated calmly, my fingers nervously winding my purse strap. "Donna's right—there is a ghost in that house."

"Oh sure," he replied with a smirk, glancing at me.

"No—really," I continued, suddenly unable to meet his question-ing gaze. "Actually, it's Donna's aunt."

His expression said he couldn't decide if I was crazy or I hon-estly did know something of which the rest of them hadn't been aware. "How do you know that?" he tested quietly, waiting for me to burst out laughing and call him a sucker.

"Because that's what I do," I said quietly instead, and he knew I was serious.

* * *

My Italian grandmother Maria bathed me in my grandfather's homemade wine when I was born, to chase the devil away. They say that, if it's a hard delivery, the devil will come to help the baby out, so it had become an Italian tradition to bathe newborns in wine. Besides, Grandma Maria never took chances. She had an Ability, too, and knew firsthand about other planes than this. Grandma Maria could sense spirits in a place, and if she spent the night there, she could talk to the ghosts in her dreams. Grandma always took care of me in that way, and it was in her kitchen that my life had begun in such a spiritual manner, when I was just one week old.

My mother believed in people having these abilities, but she didn't have them herself. She had really good instincts, but the Ability had skipped right over her, so it fell to Maria to nurture that part of me, as soon as she recognized that I could see spirits. Maria had been raised in a small Italian village before she moved to America, and she could remember certain women in the village who were special—the women you went to for specific things, like getting rid of ghosts or lifting a curse—so it really didn't take much for her to see those abilities in me, especially since she herself, and her husband's mother, had been among those people.

My father had Bohemian parents, but they died not long after I was born. They weren't Catholic, as was the maternal side, but Dad converted for Mom when he married her. Mom had been his neighbor—that's how they'd met—so he knew all about what he was getting into with her family. His family was very laid back; very open-minded and artistically centered—as you would expect. Still, he never believed in such things. Even when we went to church, he'd just sit in the car and read the paper, parked out of the way by the priests' quarters. His philosophy was that, as long as you led a good

8

life, and let others live—never hurt anyone or killed anyone or cheated anyone—then it was between you and God, without the need for a middleman.

It was with this same no-nonsense attitude that he viewed my Ability: he didn't believe in it any more than he did church, but he never prevented us from discussing it, or tried to stop my Grandma Maria from teaching me how to bring the Ability under my control. And when others found out about my Ability, he'd just play the healthy skeptic and roll his eyes, neither accepting nor dismissing the claims. Even when Maria wanted to take me to New York to help someone—even when I was only seven—he just told her that, as long as she paid for my trip, he didn't mind at all.

Dad left most of my raising to the women, in fact. He was from that time period when men raised the boys and women raised the girls. Well, he and Mom had four girls, so Dad didn't have much to do in that respect, but he did entertain us all with his accordion. As far as I know, that instrument went everywhere with him—the army even gave it its own serial number so that he could take it to Europe during World War II to relax and entertain there, as well. That's probably why he was so accepting of other customs and traditions: because he was Bohemian and full of all the artistic, relaxed stereotypes that culture brings to mind.

Grandma Maria learned what I could do when I was just 26 months old. That was when my sister was born, so I had to stay with Grandma. I was learning so-called "normal" things very quickly and had already mastered talking in complete sentences, and the day after my sister was born, Maria heard me playing and talking. After listening for a few moments, she came to realize I wasn't just childishly babbling, but was actually having a conversation. When she came into the room, she saw that I was alone.

"Mary Ann?" she whispered in a cheerful voice, speaking Italian, of course. "Who are you talking to?" She looked around, and I know now that she could sense the spirit in the room. Since she had dreamed of him the night before, she knew all along who it was, but I think she was trying to test the range of my Ability, to see if I really could see and talk to him when I was awake.

"He says he is paesano," I replied in the curt manner all children seem to have when asked something they deem obvious. Grandma Maria smiled broadly and kind of hugged herself, then started asking me all these questions to ask this man. Paesano, she told me, is the Italian word for a friend of the family so close that he is considered blood-family, and she was very happy to see him. Back then, the mail was so slow and people didn't really have phones, so it was easier for a spirit, when it died, to visit someone with an Ability who also knew its relatives; that way, that person could pass the message on. In this case, the paesano had died a day or two before and had come to Grandma Maria so she could tell his relatives living in America. Maria did this, of course, and three weeks later, the bereavement letter arrived from Italy.

She asked me so many things of him while she had the chance— things no two-year-old could either know or lie about—that she became readily convinced of the depth of my Ability. My powers were much greater than her own, and not confined to just one area. Not only could I see and talk to spirits—any spirits, unlike Maria, who had to either know the person who had died, or else one of their relatives—but I could also help them cross over into the White Light. Then there were curses, and even psychometry. In most villages, there were several women who had an Ability, and you'd go to a specific one for whatever you needed. But with me, I had it all rolled up into one. From that moment on, Maria took it upon herself to hone my Ability and to teach me how to best use it. By the time I was four, she had started taking me to funerals with her to talk to the recently

10

deceased. The family's circle of friends knew all about me by this time, so they wanted me there to ask any last-minute questions about settling earthly matters before the deceased moved on for good. That was part of it, too: Grandma Maria saw that I could help the spirits cross over into the White Light when I was at funerals, so she honed that skill so that I could do it whenever I wanted to. She called it "making the sunlight" for the dead to walk into, leaving this worldly plane behind.

"See how the sun looks?" she asked me one day at sunset, when the sun wasn't as bright as in the daytime or at dawn, and we could give it a passing gaze. "See how bright it is?"

"Yes."

"Okay, now look into the garage," she told me in Italian. "and make it bright like that in there—bright like the sun is!"

"All right." And I did it—I just could, because Grandma Maria had told me to.

"That's good," she whispered with happy awe, then she knelt down and looked me right in the eyes. "Now, whenever you see a spirit, especially one you don't like or you think is bad, or one that's asked you to help them, you make that Sunlight and send them into it."

"Okay Grandma."

She hugged me tightly, and I could feel the warmth of her holding me close, then she whispered in my ear. "When you make the sunlight, no spirit can ignore you if you tell it to walk into it, all right? So don't be afraid, okay? As long as they're walking, they can't hurt you. They have to go, because you told them to, understand?"

And none of these things do frighten me. For one thing, they seem completely natural, and we only fear what we don't really understand. But more so than that, Grandma Maria had told me not to be afraid, so I simply knew there was absolutely no reason for me to be so.

11

* * *

Ted hadn't said one word through my short admission about Grandma Maria and my abilities, but as soon as I lapsed into silence, he sort of smirked at me again and said coyly, "Can you wiggle your nose, like on Bewitched?" I was glad that was all he wanted to know —at least he didn't run off the road or anything, or snatch our daughter from the backseat and run raving into the night.

"No," I sighed with a smile. "She's a witch and she's a TV show. It doesn't work like that."

He glanced at me again, and I knew he sincerely believed me, even though he was trying to make light of it—mostly because of Amber, our daughter, in the backseat. He looked at her sleeping peacefully, then kind of whispered, "Will Amber be able to do this, too?"

I shrugged helplessly. "I really don't know."

If she could, I knew it was up to us to preserve it, as best we could, but also to let her live a normal life. In hindsight, I sometimes feel as though my grandmother used me a lot of the time, dragging me from funeral to funeral—starting when I was just four years old—so I didn't want to raise my own children in the same fashion. Ultimately I'm thankful that my family helped me perfect—and not simply lose—my Abilities, but I knew there had to be a middle ground between teaching a child and exploiting a child.

All children can do these things to a certain extent, but the same things frighten most adults, so the child learns to turn it off—to fear it, as the adults clearly do. That's why I say, when all is said and done, that I'm so lucky to have had Grandma Maria. She kept me using the Abilities, so they got stronger and stronger. There was one point, from when I was about 15 to 18, where I didn't like having that kind of power anymore, so I had to teach myself how to turn it on and off. Otherwise I would have just kept seeing ghosts, and a teen has enough things to worry about without having to help spirits all the time! The mind is amazingly powerful, so when I told it I didn't want to see or hear anything, it all just went away, like switching off a radio. The Ability was still there, just not being used—if I kept it on all the time, I'd probably go crazy.

"All right," Ted agreed. "So what are you going to do about Donna's aunt?"

I shrugged again. "I guess I'll have to get Donna alone and talk about it. I just thought, you know, if I started to tell people outside the family, you should be the first to hear it."

He smiled thankfully. "Weird, isn't it?"

"Yeah," I admitted. "It can get pretty weird."

* * *

What had happened with Donna and her husband, Bobby, was actually pretty ordinary. I had known, just from being in the house, that there was a female spirit there. I would have said something if it had seemed dangerous or wanted to hurt anyone—especially their little girl, since some spirits do not like children—but I knew it was Donna's aunt, so I didn't mention a thing.

Grandma Maria had always told me not to tell anyone about what I could do, even though she was always telling people. Later I understood why. When children talk like that, adults get angry with them, and Grandma Maria was trying to prepare me for when I'd be on my own. If I kept telling people, and they kept getting angry, it would indirectly teach me to turn the Ability off for good. It was all right to mention it around people who believed and wouldn't become upset, but I couldn't blab around just anyone. Bobby was Ted's friend from work, and I didn't know Donna too well either, so I didn't say anything about her aunt being in the house. Most ghosts want to be known, however, and Donna's aunt was no different.

We were all sitting quietly, talking and playing cards in the dining room, when there came a horrendous crash from the kitchen, as if every shelf had simultaneously collapsed, spilling all the pots and pans and dinnerware onto the floor. We all jumped, but Donna just laughed.

"I'm not getting up," she said. "It's nothing."

"Nothing!" Bobby cried. "It sounded like the whole cupboard came off the wall!"

"Get up and see," she told him, winking at me. I realized that Donna had witnessed something like this many times before and had simply become accustomed to it, though she didn't necessarily know what was going on.

A second later, Bobby returned to the room shaking his head, his face the perfect image of confusion and bafflement.

"There's nothing wrong," he declared and plopped back down into his chair with a huff.

"Told you," Donna declared playfully, then glanced at Ted and I to bring us into the conversation. "It's like when I'm washing the floors, and I'll go back over to the bucket, only it will have moved."

Donna sat back decisively. "Bobby, I keep telling you there's a ghost in this house."

"Oh, right," he replied incredulously with a nervous laugh.

His response didn't surprise me a bit. That's how most people react to ghost stories, which is why Grandma Maria taught me not to mention anything to strangers. The first time I learned that lesson firsthand was shortly after I'd started school. I went to St. Francis de Sales, a Catholic school in Parma, Ohio, and I remember one of the nuns, Sister Mary, was the first person to get angry with me and tell me to stop.

It was recess, and I'd gone to the bathroom with my friend Lizzie. As we were returning to the playground, I glanced over at her and saw this really negative male entity walking along behind her. I saw this spirit twice, and though it never hurt her, it did affect her, because both days she was moody and didn't want to play.

"Hey, Lizzie...?" I started to ask, but when she looked at me, I remembered what Grandma had said. I was afraid for her, and I wanted to let her know, but I changed the subject instead. "I'll meet you by the swings, okay?"

"Uh huh," she agreed morosely and wandered off across the playground. Sister Mary was standing by the doors, so I thought I should tell her about the man following Lizzie, since she was a nun.

"Sister?" I said bashfully once Lizzie was out of earshot. "There's a bad man following Lizzie." She looked across the playground at the girl, and for a moment, I thought she knew what I was talking about, but then she smiled back at me.

"Don't worry. It's her guardian angel."

Back then the walls were covered with pictures of angels—beautiful angels with halos and wings, all hugging little children—so I knew that the man behind Lizzie was not an angel. Since then I've also learned I can't see guardian angels, because I can't see any spirit that has gone into the Light, then come back, or is only of the Light to begin with. Regardless of that, even when I was a schoolgirl, I knew it was no angel following Lizzie around, but what was I to do? Argue about what an angel is with a nun?

Instead, I dropped it, and by the time we got back to the classroom after recess, the spirit had faded away, so I just let the whole thing go. Then, three weeks later, Lizzie was in a bad mood again, sitting off by herself at recess, watching us jump rope, but not participating in any way. When I looked over at her, I saw that bad man again standing behind her. I, of course, ran over to tell Sister Mary again.

"Sister Mary? There's that bad man standing behind Lizzie again, and I don't think he's an angel." She looked over, but again saw nothing. This time she bent down and looked at me sternly.

"Now you stop this, Mary Ann!" she admonished. "Stop it, or I'll send you to see the priest. You're not going to make your First Communion talking like this, are you?" That scared me badly, because she'd not only threatened to send me straight to the priest without seeing the principal first, she'd also told me I'd miss one of a Catholic's most important rites of passage.

I went straight home and told my mother about it, terrified that the Ability would prevent my First Communion, and she sat me down and said very calmly, "Mary Ann, this is why you can't go around telling everyone about your power. You have to be very careful." She explained to me that, when Grandma told people, it was because those people had asked, or at least understood, so they were ready and willing to hear about ghosts. Most people, she told me, didn't understand such things and didn't want to understand, so they would get angry.

"It's better to not tell anyone, okay?" she soothed. "Unless they ask."

"But what about the man behind Lizzie?" I wondered. The root of my concern wasn't so much for me, but for Lizzie.

"Honey, if you can get rid of him," my mother said, standing and straightening my hair around my face, "then get rid of him. But if you can't, then just leave him alone."

As it turned out, I never got the chance to try, because I never saw that bad man again—from then, all the way up to when we graduated from high school. I never found out who he was or what he wanted from Lizzie, but I did learn to keep my mouth shut in the future, unless I was asked or knew the person believed in the Ability.

That's how I dealt with Donna's revelation about her ghost that moved things around and made a lot of noise. I just sat with my playing cards and smiled, sharing the nervous mirth of those around me. I saw that Donna would readily talk—and may want my help—but not with her husband there. I let the subject drop, but some of my shyness melted away, maybe because of the way Ted glanced at me the rest of the night. I knew it was time to let my own growing circle of family and friends in on the secret, to a certain degree.

I never advertised—and still don't. If I found out someone needed help, I'd size them up, then offer, and my Ability spread by word of mouth. Telling Ted kind of brought me out into the open, and I found myself doing something for someone at least once a month. It was like that for about 20 years, in which time Ted and I had two kids, as well as foster children, and I ran a few businesses, including a diaper service and a dog grooming salon. Then, in 1989, I did a radio spot about my work, which I imagined to be a kind of public interest story—but it changed everything.

Pretty soon I was swamped with friends, or friends of friends, and even strangers who needed help, and since it began to take up so much of my time, I had to start asking for a little bit of money, to cover my expenses from all the driving, plus my time and what-have-you. My primary concern was to help both the living and the dead, and it still is the only thing that motivates me, but by 1991 there were so many people calling for help, that I was basically forced into making it a business. Other people sell their talents, and if I was going to do this as much as people needed me to, then I would need to put a price on my talents, as well.

It was a big departure from my old lifestyle. Before—for the two years when I'd been too afraid to tell Ted—I'd just tell him that I was going to visit Grandma Maria for a couple of hours. He never knew why I was going away all the time, but he never asked either. I suppose he imagined it was family stuff. Mostly it was funerals that I'd go to with Grandma, like when I was young, but occasionally there'd be a negative spirit in someone's house or just a relative who hadn't managed to cross over, as in Donna's case. Those kinds of spirits really only want to hang out, watch their loved ones, and that kind of thing—most people don't need any help until they run across something negative, or at least something frustrated and confused, such that it starts making a nuisance of itself.

* * *

Ted pulled into the driveway and put the car in park. Amber stirred in the backseat, but didn't wake from her doze. "So what about Donna's aunt? Can you get her into the Light?"

I nodded slowly. "Probably. There have only been a few I couldn't get into the Light, but that's because they were so negative." I chuckled lightly. "I guess Grandma was wrong about that. I mean, about if I told them they'd have to go. Anyway," I shrugged, opening my door and starting to step out, "even those, I've at least gotten out of the house, or back to wherever they came from."

Ironically, I never did talk to Donna's aunt. In fact, I never told her about the ghost being in the house at all. Her spirit wasn't malicious or negative in any way; she was simply trying to make her presence known. But Donna never brought it up again, and so even when we were alone, I wouldn't break my personal oath and tell her about it; if she'd have wanted to talk, that would have been one thing, but I wasn't about to broach the subject myself. Some people are fine with ghosts, as long as they don't hurt anything or anyone, so who am I to tell those people what's best or to get rid of the spirit? If it had been a very negative entity, I would have done something without telling her, but it was only her aunt.

Ted grinned and looked around at the darkness before he opened

Amber's door and helped her out, and I knew what he was thinking, his eyes searching for ghosts in all the shadows. Amber had been unaware of the whole conversation, since she was only seven months old and she'd been asleep, and we decided to keep it that way, rather than making her feel pushed into using the Ability like I had. Ted and I decided to keep our daughters away from it until they were old enough to decide for themselves what they wanted to do.

We had two girls, and when Amber was 17 and Tara 14, we sat them down and told them. In our effort to protect them from being used like I had, however, we had tipped the scale in the other direction, and they had been raised—by outside influences—to fear the Abilities they knew they had. Amber is willing to use her Ability, though she can only do what Grandma Maria had been able to do. Tara, on the other hand, is a lot like me, but she's terrified of what she can do, so she chooses not to. I wish I could go back and change that, because I could certainly use the help now. Unfortunately, they've seen too many movies, and the entire concept frightens Tara badly.

I'd never been scared, and as I got older, I learned that people's spirits have the same personalities as the people did in life. If they were grouchy and annoying in life, then their spirits will be the same way. A lot of the time, it's body language, just like with the living. If I talk to a spirit, and it shrugs or rolls its eyes, then I know it has an attitude and that I'll have to be that much stronger. When you see it that way—without Hollywood's glitz and special effects—it becomes quite mundane. They may be dead, but they're just like people; they behave exactly as any stranger you run into on the street. Even so, it was tough to convince the girls. Not as tough as it was to convince my Aunt Susanne, however.

Quite a few years after trying to convince our daughters about my abilities and of their harmless nature, my aging Aunt Susanne moved into an addition on the back of our house after undergoing triple-bypass surgery. She didn't expect to live much longer, so she wanted to be near someone who could care for her and prevent her from dying alone. She'd never had children of her own, and with the number of foster children Ted and I had cared for over the years, I figured we could handle old Aunt Susanne.

Since I was always in and out helping people with spirits, I soon realized that I would have to sit down and tell her what was going on and where I kept disappearing to. She never actually denied that I could do what I said I could do, but she remained ever skeptical, right up until the end.

"Be nice to me," I remember joking, when I told her, "because I'm the last person on earth you're going to talk to!"

After 11 years, she had congestive heart-failure, and she was quickly hospitalized. Now, there were a handful of things Aunt Susanne was truly terrified of: having a stroke, being on life-support, and the state getting her money. Years before her second hospitalization, she tried to take care of the last issue by giving me power of attorney. We kept trying to explain to her that such a thing was only good if she was alive, and that if she really wanted to get one up on the state, she should let me change all of her accounts over to my name. Of course, she would hear nothing of the sort, and so she lay, quite literally on her deathbed, with all of her accounts threatening to topple at any moment into probate.

At two in the morning, after she'd been hospitalized for heart failure, the hospital called and told me that my aunt had just had a stroke, paralyzing her left side. They assured me that she was fine—that all her vitals were just dandy, with the obvious exceptions—but we decided we should go down anyway, since she was probably terrified at one of her nightmares having come true. She needed us there to assure her that she wasn't going to turn into a vegetable.

Twenty minutes later, over a wake-up cup of coffee, the phone rang again. It was the hospital: The nurse was very upset and very sorry, but Aunt Susanne had just passed away. As I was discussing how this turn of events had occurred—from vitals being fine to sudden death—I glanced into the next room, and sure enough, I found out the nurse on the phone was telling the truth. Standing in the dining room, peeking at us from behind the china hutch, was my aunt's spirit.

I hung up the phone and said flatly, "She's dead. I guess that means the state will get a cut of her money after all."

"What?" Ted asked. Being unable to see her, he couldn't understand why I'd bring up such a thing at that time.

"Yeah," I said. "Since she didn't change the accounts into my name, I guess all her money will go to probate."

"I know that!" Ted declared. His face hinted at a certain amount of betrayal, that I would speak not of her death, but simply of money. I glanced into the dining room, but Aunt Susanne was gone.

We had just returned to the bedroom to finish getting dressed when the phone rang again. Ted shot me an odd look, like I knew something I wasn't sharing.

"What?" he shrieked into the phone, after discovering that it was the hospital again. "Alive? She just came back to life?"

He cut me a look that said we'd placed her under the care of the wrong people.

"She what?" he cried, even more incredulously. "We'll be right down."

It turned out that Aunt Susanne had been dead, officially, according to two nurses and a doctor. They'd called to tell me, then they'd gone back in to take off the oxygen mask and prepare her for our arrival. As soon as the nurse took off the mask, Aunt Susanne apparently gasped, then leaped from the bed, pushed one nurse over, hit

21

another in the chin, and a third in the shoulder, at which point the poor nurse who'd taken off the mask lost control of her bodily functions. It took three orderlies to wrestle this woman back into her bed and strap her down. And remember: She was a stroke victim. The entire left side of her body had been paralyzed (and still was), yet she had managed to leap out of bed—over the guardrails—without so much as a scratch on her, land on her feet without stumbling, and had injured three nurses.

I knew exactly why, and I told Ted so on the way to the hospital.

"I said all that about her money for a reason," I explained.

"Yeah?" he wondered. "Why?"

"Because she was dead, and she was standing in the dining room. I just thought she should know that her stubbornness over those accounts had finally beaten her."

Ted glanced at me, waiting for my conclusion.

"I guess it worked," I finished. "She must've jumped back into her body!"

"You think?" he asked with disbelief.

"What else?" I replied, and he shrugged in agreement. "But now, this morning, I have to go and sign those accounts over to my name."

"Mary—"

"No, Ted," I said. "After this, she's not going to die until I've done that. That's how stubborn and determined she is, isn't it?"

Ted actually giggled. "I guess so."

When we got there, Aunt Susanne was in a coma, but we stayed with her for the rest of the night, until it was morning and the banks would be open, at which point I left and took care of the business at hand. Sometime after nine, I returned and said with a sigh, "Okay, it's done."

Ted was glad, mainly because he'd been sitting there for so long, listening to every doctor and nurse that came in explain to him what

22

had happened, or at least theorize about it. None of them knew her like I had, though, and I had to laugh to myself. It was nothing medical or miraculous—it was a simple fact that Aunt Susanne had been so determined that the state wasn't going to take any of her money, she had brought herself back to life.

I told Ted it was done, then I glanced over at her and saw her spirit standing there, outside her body.

"Should you tell her?" Ted wondered.

"She heard me," I replied, looking right at her. "And she's dead now."

Ted glanced over, and though he couldn't see her spirit, he nodded, because he knew I wasn't lying.

"What?" Aunt Susanne's spirit suddenly piped up, glaring at me. "How do you know I'm dead?"

I really don't think she expected me to reply. "I told you I could see you when you were dead."

"Oh my Lord!" she gasped. "You can see ghosts!"

I smirked at her. "I told you to be nice to me! Now what's all this nonsense that went on here? I saw you last night, too, in the dining room."

"But I was hiding!"

"Yeah. Behind the hutch. So why'd you come back?"

"State's not getting my money!" she said as if it were obvious, and I suppose it was.

Then I asked her about the nurses and why she'd beaten them up—and she couldn't remember a thing about it. She certainly wasn't the type of person that would have done something of that nature, so I suppose it didn't really surprise me that she couldn't recall doing anything. Must be the product of jumping back into your body.

My aunt didn't say anything about her near-death experience, which in hindsight is unfortunate, because I cannot see into the

White Light. I have no idea what's on the other side—I can't even talk to the spirits who have been there, so there isn't even any hearsay evidence for me to consider. Once I did have myself hypnotically regressed, just to see if there was anything to the whole reincarnation phenomenon, and that may be the closest I'll ever come to any definitive answers—at least until I cross over myself.

The regression actually took me back through several lives, and every time I went far enough back to be at the end of the previous life—between lives, in other words—I found myself in this glistening, foggy white place. All around me I could hear voices talking, as if I were at a cafe or in a train station, but I couldn't distinguish any specific words or phrases. People were talking, but they weren't talking to me, and they were just out of earshot. I remember it was very comfortable there—I felt unencumbered and completely at ease, but clearly it wasn't enough, because I kept leaving the white foggy area to enter a new life.

I have come to understand that you need to go into the White Light; you need to experience the comfort of the foggy area before you can go any further spiritually, either as pure energy or through reincarnation. For some, it may be a great lesson, a learning process that they have to pass to move on, each time with more and more of their questions slowly answered. But there are different steps. Someone like Mother Teresa—I don't think she'll have much left to learn or any reason to come back. Maybe she would want to continue her angelic lifestyle as someone else—not to teach herself, but to teach us. Maybe she'll prefer to simply stay wherever heaven is; it all comes down to free will. Nobody has to enter the White Light, so it could be assumed that nobody has to be reincarnated either.

I have let all kinds into the White Light: nice old men, sweet old ladies, your usual assortment of minor jerks and pains in the ass, but also murderers, rapists, and pedophiles. I have sent all of these types of people into the White Light, so I have to believe there's someone on the other side with a clipboard, standing there directing traffic. I can't imagine for an instant that all of these people would go to the same place. Perhaps the foggy area is simply the waiting room; maybe reincarnation is not up to us. Maybe God decides who will be born again, and thus that spirit never enters heaven or hell, but simply returns and continues living. Such questions have led to a sort of open-minded attitude I keep about all of this—and not just religious matters. Sometimes there are more questions than answers. As soon as I think I may have figured something out, something else comes along to turn it on its ear. I suppose I am doing God's work, but it is not necessary for me to understand exactly how it is that I can do what I do.

One thing I am certain of is that, no matter how good you are, no one who goes into the Light is handed wings and a halo to become an angel. Angels are a different life form, to put it mundanely. They are created just as we are, and you're either one to begin with, or you're never one. Not even Mother Teresa, who definitely had angelic qualities, can become a full-fledged angel. Although (and here come the questions again, hot on the heels of anything close to an answer) I do think it is possible for angels to incarnate themselves and work among us. In that case, it wouldn't surprise me if Mother Teresa were one of these angels, but the basic premise still stands intact: She didn't die and become an angel; she was one to begin with.

Of course, if you mention angels, you have to mention the opposite side of the coin, which is also very real. There are demons—or such negative energies, at least, that I have to think of them as demons—and those I can see. Even so, in the whole time that I've been doing this, I've run across maybe 15 really nasty entities that I would call demons. They're not common, no matter what

25

Hollywood would have us believe, and they don't just decide to go for a joyride on earth. Usually they are called up by something or someone dabbling in black witchcraft or satanism, or whatever you want to call it. But to give these things credit—as little as they deserve—they never physically fight me on being sent away or back to whatever cesspool they crawled from.

Obviously, these things do not get sent into the White Light. They wouldn't go anyway, and I can't force them in any more than I can force your grandmother in. I give them the option to simply leave the home they're haunting or go back where they came from. For the longest time, I had no image of where that was—I just knew some went away—then Hollywood, ironically, supplied what I feel is an appropriate image, and is the one which I now use to banish them.

In the film Ghost, toward the end, there is a scene in which an entity is caught in a black, oily quagmire—a representation of the doorway to hell, we imagine. Well, whatever it was, it worked for me, and now if I come across something so negative that I know it was never of the White Light to begin with, I envision this black, oily spot, much like I create the White Light for normal spirits, and the demon will go into that. Perhaps I patch into the thing's latent negative energy and simply create a negative place. Who knows? And ultimately, who cares? Just as long as it goes. The overwhelming message is that it is not necessary for me to see or know the "other side" like that—I must simply send these spirits and entities on, and God will take care of the rest.

Funerals

The Old Lady and the Backwards Dress

It was the Wednesday before Thanksgiving, and I was in the middle of preparing some festive delicacy when the phone rang. I considered letting the machine pick it up, but finally changed my mind and walked over, hooking the receiver with my pinky.

"Hello?"

"Hi, is this Mary Ann?"

"Yeah..." I knew it had to be about a ghost, since I didn't recognize the voice.

"Well, my grandmother just died, and I heard you sometimes attended the funerals...?"

It was a rhetorical question; I sighed and scratched my head with a hooked left hand, which still had turkey fat dripping off it.

"Sure," I said nicely. "How old was your grandmother?"

"Ninety-six."

I didn't mean to chuckle, but I did. "Oh, I don't think she'll stick around. You don't need me to come out there."

"But...we do," she replied adamantly. Usually that translates to the fact that the deceased person has hidden away something valuable, and the living don't know where it was. While such curiosities are enticing, they are ultimately unimportant, in the grand sense. My

27

purpose is to ensure that spirits cross over into the White Light, not to be a hired treasure hunter. Still, I felt an obligation. I'd found little velvet bags full of diamonds before, and they went a long way toward helping an otherwise poverty-stricken family get on its feet again.

"Well, when's the visitation?" I asked, preferring to do my work when the event wasn't so well-orchestrated, as is the actual funeral itself. If the spirit was a really mean person and the family wants to make absolutely sure that it's gone from this world, then I will attend both the visitation and the funeral, but for something such as this—making last-minute arrangements that weren't in the will or getting maps to buried treasure—the visitations are just fine.

"The visitation's Friday," she answered, her hesitation denoting that she knew what she was asking me to do. I realize the day after Thanksgiving is not, officially, part of the holiday, but everyone—including me—views it as such. I sighed.

"Look, there's no way your grandmother is going to stick around. Is your grandfather still alive—her husband?"

"No, he died about 10 years back."

"Then there's no way," I said definitively, determining that the conversation was over. "She'll see her husband in the Light and go straight to him."

"But it's not about that," the woman said, her voice tainted with a deep, nervous desire.

"Did she leave money hidden somewhere?" I assumed.

"No, not that I know about," the woman replied curiously, and I knew I had inadvertently put her hotter on the trail of my being there. Still, it did also work to peak my own curiosity—what could possibly be so important that this woman would want me there? She obviously wasn't worried about her grandmother hanging around; nor was she looking for a buried jar of quarters, so to speak. It had to be something less tangible; more meaningful.

Finally I sighed and nodded to myself. "All right," I agreed. "I'll come out and see what I can do. Where is it?"

The young woman passed on the information, then allowed me to return to preparing the Thanksgiving feast. Ted would be watching football anyway, I figured, so I may as well get out of the house for a couple of hours.

* * *

When I got to the funeral home, I immediately saw the spirit of the 96-year-old woman, perched atop her casket, chewing her teeth with displeasure, as older women always seem to do. Spirits always attend their visitations and funerals—it's only natural. They want to see who turned up and whether they're really sad, and generally spy on the gathering. Not to scare people, or put them on edge at such services, but the spirit of the deceased is always there, right by the casket. Sometimes the spirit stands behind it, sometimes it sits on the end of it, sometimes it sits on the raised lid and dangles its feet over its body. It's the perfect place to be, since people facing the deceased have their backs to the rest of the room; it's the only place from which a spirit can see the faces of the mourners. Sometimes they just wander around, checking out the flowers and arrangements, but they're always there somewhere.

Whenever I enter a funeral home, I try to make overtures to the spirit so that it knows I can see and talk to it, and can then explain to it why a stranger is crashing its funeral. It had just occurred to me that the old woman was in a hospital gown—usually spirits are in the clothes they're wearing in the casket—when the granddaughter caught my arm.

"Hi!" she said cheerily. "I'm so glad you came. This is my mother," she added, grabbing a woman by the arm as she walked past. The mother smiled a bit hesitantly, then shook my hand.

"Okay," I smiled after the introductions. "Well, she is here, sitting right atop her casket, and I think she knows I can see her." Both of the women in front of me squinted over at the casket, but of course saw nothing. "Shall we go find out whatever it is that you need?" I suggested.

"First, let me tell you," the granddaughter said secretively, pulling me aside. "About eight years ago, she had a growth in her intestines, so we had surgery done and got it removed."

"Uh huh," I said, following her so far.

"Well, it kept her alive, obviously, but then the growth came back earlier this year. This time we decided to just let nature take its course."

"Okay..."

"And she died—obviously."

"All right. So what do you need?"

"We just want to know," the mother cut in, "whether she's angry at us for not having the second surgery done. I mean, our choice did kill her..."

I could see the assumed guilt written all over their faces and saw now why the granddaughter had been so adamant on the phone. It was sort of like the reaction to suicides—in which the family is convinced it was murder—in that they simply needed to assuage their own feelings of blame for the death. It is completely understandable, and sometimes, relieving that burden is worth more to people than little bags of diamonds. Sometimes.

"All right," I understood, and led them over to the casket, which was thankfully free of visitors at that point. I'm never sure how many of the people at visitations know who I am or what I'm doing, so I'm always careful when I talk to the spirits. I have to watch my hand motions especially, because to an outsider it looks for all the world like I'm talking to thin air. Facial expressions are a lot more difficult for me to suppress, but I try. Luckily, communication is telepathic, so I don't have to speak out loud.

Well, we got the first few things out of the way—last goodbyes and sentimentalities—and then I turned to the question at hand, asking her if she was upset that her family had basically let her die.

"God no!" she declared, chewing her teeth and sucking her gums in that ever-annoying old-person way. She kind of shot them a look of slight disgust, and for a moment I was confused, but then she went on. "They should've let me die the first time! I've been ready for years!"

I passed the response along, and the two women sighed with visible relief, glancing at the body, then at the air above the casket where I'd said the grandmother was sitting. It still kind of bothered me that she was wearing a hospital gown—spirits always seem to find clothes somewhere—but it was wasn't that important, so I let it go. The two women passed on a few more goodbyes, which were reciprocated by the old woman, and then my job was done, so I turned to go. Just as I'd taken a step away, I heard that old lady suck her gums at me.

"Girly!" she croaked. "Girly!"

I turned back around slowly. "Yes?"

"Well, I just think you better tell them that my dress is on backwards," she said haughtily. I took a few steps back to the casket and looked down at her body. She was wearing a blue, floral print dress that buttoned up the front, and it looked fine to me.

"Are you sure?" I asked, which was a mistake.

"It's my dress, girly," she snapped. "Don't you think I know?"

"All right," I shrugged. I debated whether or not to say anything. The conversation had been, as always, completely silent to everyone else in the room, and it really didn't matter one way or the other about her dress—dead is dead, and nobody alive seemed to care.

Still, it seemed really important to her, so I turned to the granddaughter and whispered, "She says her dress is on backwards."

The young woman's face blanched. "No!"

"That's what she says," I replied, glancing over at the old woman. She was chewing her teeth furiously now, her arms crossed and her lips pursed. She could, of course, hear every word we said.

The granddaughter discreetly walked up to the casket and reached down to check the neckline of the dress, and sure enough, the tag popped out. Her face flushed in embarrassment as she quickly tucked it back in.

"Well," she said, turning to me to throw her some sort of life ring. "We can just get the funeral director to quickly flip it around, right? We'll have to clear the room—"

I was shaking my head in negation. "That dress can't be turned around."

"Why not?" she gasped.

"It's ruined. They cut them up the back so they can clothe the body. I mean, they're called stiffs for a reason," I finished in a hushed voice. Grandma was not too happy with my announcement; she looked as angry as the granddaughter did guilty.

"Well, ask her what she wants to wear and I'll get my husband to run home and get it, then we can change her clothes."

It was a fair enough proposition, so I glanced at the old woman for her answer. She was sitting there tapping her chin with her index finger, going through all the motions of a serious decision. At least now I knew why she was wearing her hospital gown, not the backwards dress that she had on in the casket.

"The navy blue dress?" the granddaughter wondered, not yet having received a reply.

"No," Grandma mused. "That got fuzzy over the years." I passed on the reply, so the granddaughter tried again.

"The pastel print dress?"

"Never liked it," came the response.

"The polka-dot dress?"

"Makes me look fat."

At that point, it hit me how ludicrous this was. The woman was, frankly, dead. What did it matter? Nobody had come to the visitation to check on her fashion sense, and nobody was going to care if she looked fat! All the old biddy was doing was unnecessarily stressing out her granddaughter, who clearly felt guilty about the old woman's death in the first place and certainly wanted her funeral, at least, to go according to Grandma's plans.

"Look," I finally said to the old lady. "Just pick a dress. This is not that big of a deal, and you're just upsetting your granddaughter! As a matter of fact, this one looks fine." Then it occurred to me. "Actually, I'm just going to tell her you said that and stop her worrying."

Of course, I wouldn't have flat out lied, but some spirits, just like the people they were when they were alive, only understand compromise when you threaten to play hardball with them.

Well, Grandma thought about it for a few seconds, then grudgingly said, "Okay, I guess you're right—but just make sure everyone knows I didn't dress myself!"

"Oh, I don't think anyone will imagine you hopped up and slipped that dress on by yourself," I replied.

"She says it's fine," I told the granddaughter, cutting the old woman one last, nasty glance. "She says not to worry about it, that it looks fine."

"Really?"

"Yeah," I said honestly. "Really. She doesn't want you worrying over something so trivial."

The old lady snuffed out a disgusted chuckle, but kept quiet, and finally I was allowed to leave.

A Last Confession

I walked into the funeral home and, as usual, made my way to the casket to gain the attention of the spirit. Sometimes that is easier said than done, as I can feel the eyes of the family upon me, wondering who this is that has come to pay her respects. Other times, the person who called me will intercept me and drag me off to offer some advice or words of wisdom—often helpful, but still...

Fortunately, this time the granddaughter who had called me was engaged in conversation and didn't notice my arrival, and the spirit—her grandfather—was not standing near his casket, but was over to one side, looking at some of the floral arrangements. They really were some of the most beautiful I had ever seen, and I could completely understand why the man was taking a closer look; after all, like I say so often: As alive, so dead.

I scooted up to a position next to him, and he kind of glanced at me to see who I was. I looked into his eyes, which gave him a start, but then he obviously thought it was dumb luck on my part—until I said, "Hi. Beautiful, aren't they?"

He sort of gaped for a moment, then his face washed with relief, and he sighed heavily. "You can see me!" he gasped. "And talk to me! Oh, thank God!"

I had to chuckle and point out, "You've only been dead for two days—how can you be that lonely already?"

"No," he smirked back. "I just need to—"

At that point, the granddaughter came over and took my arm. She'd probably seen my expressions from across the room—no matter how careful I am, they still slip out from time to time—and now eyed the air before us curiously.

"Thank you for coming," she said.

"No problem," I nodded, then leaned in and whispered. "He's standing right in front of us."

Most often, that sort of thing surprises people. At funerals it's easier, because the living know who the dead is, but when it's a spirit in a house, the revelation has a sense akin to the police finding a peephole drilled through your bathroom wall. People often feel somehow betrayed; spied upon. It only figures, I suppose. At funerals, the people simply don't know how to react. They know how they'll look conversing with the air—especially when they can't hear the replies themselves—and usually just end up with a stiff back, afraid to move for fear of running into their dearly departed.

"Why did she want you here?" the man asked, nerves crowding the edges of his voice as he realized that my appearance and abilities were not accidental.

"So, what did you need to ask him?" I relayed to the granddaughter.

"Oh," the woman said, still a bit shaken. "Umm… really just one part of his will. He said we should sell his house, but he didn't say what he wanted done with all of his stuff—like his knife collection."

The man actually chuckled, and I had to concur his sentiment, but at the same time, I had to sympathize with the young woman wanting to do right.

"She can do what she wants with it!" he declared—a bit more relieved by the question than seemed natural. "If nobody wants anything, they can sell it. I don't mind. That scrimshaw knife's probably worth a couple of hundred bucks, though," he added secretively.

I passed the information on, and she came back with a few more questions along similar lines, and then seemed to be done with the whole thing. Her face had that tint of a recently lifted burden to it, and I was about to leave when the man spoke again.

"Just a minute," he said, as soon as his granddaughter had gone off to greet more relatives. "I have something important I want to tell her—and my wife."

"What's that?" I asked, ready to call the young woman back over.

"No—hold on," he asked, so I just listened instead. "You see the front row of people sitting there?"

"Yeah."

"Okay, that first woman is my wife."

"Uh huh."

"Next to her is my brother... then my sister-in-law..."

"Okay..."

"Then my neighbor. He built his house about a month after we built ours, and we've lived as neighbors for 40 years now."

"Oh? That's pretty neat—"

"And then next to him is his wife."

"Yeah," I sighed, not really needing a rundown of who's who at his funeral.

"Then next to her is her son."

"Yup."

"Well, that's also my son."

I gaped with understanding. "You've got to be kidding me?"

"Nope."

"You didn't...?"

"Yup."

"Your neighbor...?"

"Yup."

"Oh boy," I sighed. "And she's the only one who knows?"

"Right."

"So what can I do about it?"

"Well," he shrugged, giving me a burdened gaze. "I think my wife should know."

Now you have to understand, when I do these things, most people don't believe that I'm actually talking to a spirit, since they can't see or hear one and since I don't even have to talk out loud to communicate with the deceased. After the usual rigmarole of "test" questions to prove to them who the spirit is—and if it really exists—the family often comes around and realizes that I'm telling them things that only the spirit—or family—could know. The thing is, funerals are not the best place to go through such a song and dance, especially if the declaration is going to be a bombshell like the one this gentleman had just issued. I mean, I've even been asked by spirits to escort so and so out of the funeral home because they told so and so they never wanted to see them again, even at their funerals. I always refuse—I'm not a bodyguard or bouncer for the silly whims of ghosts. Nor am I the confessor of their sins to an already grieving family.

"Let me ask you this…" I replied tactfully. "You have three daughters, and one granddaughter who is 18. The daughters are all happily married—is there any chance of your son marrying your granddaughter?"

"God no!" he gasped, since his illegitimate child must have been nearly 40.

"Then we're not going to worry about it," I replied coolly, but decisively. "If there's no chance of two-headed babies, we don't need to bring it up now that you're dead."

"You don't think I have to say something?" he checked uncertainly.

"No!" I answered without hesitation.

"Will I still get into heaven?" he wondered, glancing at the White Light. The oval to the other side is always there, throughout the whole funeral, and the spirit can see into it the whole time and hear those that have passed before it calling it over. That must be their job, once they've crossed over—to call their relatives in as well. I've let murderers and rapists into that Light, so I didn't think an adulterer would be denied entry. Still, having let even murderers in, I have to believe St. Peter really is just across the way with a clipboard, so this man would have had a few questions to answer first.

"Look," I said. "Just go through the Light, and I'm sure you'll be fine."

"Yeah?" he double-checked, glancing at his wife, his neighbor, and his son.

"Yeah," I said adamantly.

He nodded regretfully, but understood that I was right—it was not the kind of revelation you brought up after you were dead, when the people involved couldn't honestly react to you on a personal level, no matter that I was there to serve as a go-between.

"All right," he finally agreed, then began to wander back over to his casket. "Well, thanks anyway, for everything else."

"No problem," I said, and caught myself just as I returned his departing wave.

Setting the Record Straight

Many of the funeral home rendezvous are designed for the purpose of gaining some form of hidden wealth; not so many as to be called common, but still quite a few. I don't mean that to sound so greedy, but the pragmatist in all of us says coolly that, if Grandpa died, and we know he had a stash, why not ask him where it is? For some people, the "stash" is nothing more than the location of the will, but for some it is more specifically where the money is hidden, or the key to the safe-deposit box. Those kinds are actually rather fun, bringing out the romantic child in me who's still searching for hidden treasure in the backyard. In that way, I've led families to hidden drawers, removable wall panels, bricks that come out of foundations, fancy bookcases with a false book or two—all of which reveal something, from rolls of cash to bearer bonds to precious stones—and even once to that small velvet bag of diamonds.

Of course, the moment the family uncovers the hidden treasures, they want to know how their departed one got it—where it came from, whether it was stolen, who'd come after them if it were found out they had it—but by that time, the funeral is usually done, the deceased has crossed over, and it's far too late for me to help them get answers to any further questions.

Perhaps the strangest—and most selfish—of these I came across was a man, years after the owner of some property had died, who called and asked me to help him "check out the land" before he bought it. At first it was just that I didn't want to drive all the way out there simply to see whether the property was haunted, so I declined, pointing out that, if he bought it and it was haunted, then I could come out. He didn't like that, and to cut a long story short, he'd heard that the old man who had died had secreted a large amount of money somewhere on the property, and really, all the man who called me wanted to do was find out where it was so he could take it, then not buy the property from the family.

I staunchly declined.

I will help the family locate a deceased family member's loot, but I will not help a stranger take money from under their noses, unbeknownst to them. I won't lie to the spirit's family, no matter how problematic a response may be. There are times I opt not to tell people things—like the case of the guy with his illegitimate child—but that's not lying to them, that's saving the family in some way.

The only other time I've really withheld the truth from relatives regarded an unambitious family whose patriarch had recently died. Again, the granddaughter called me. She and her husband had lived in her grandfather's house along with her mother. Her mother had been unable to hold a job and had constantly moved in and out of her parents' house her whole life. The granddaughter and her husband had jobs, but it was very low-paying work, the likes of which would never amount to anything and certainly wouldn't allow them to simply move away after the death of the homeowner.

Now, this granddaughter had two other sisters who were considerably older—the granddaughter that had called me was sort of a late-life surprise—and those other two never felt any real ties to their younger sibling. For one thing, both of them had married and gone on to good jobs, with homes of their own, and probably looked down on the rest of the family—their mother and little sister—as the weak link in their heritage. At least, that was the impression I got from the granddaughter and also when I met them at the funeral home. I had been called to see if Grandpa had any last wishes that weren't in his will, which had specified that his house and belongings be sold off and that the proceeds would be split equally among the three grand-daughters.

I finally got some time alone near the casket—and the old man's spirit—to squeeze him for some real answers. He reiterated what was in the will; the three sisters were off to one side arguing, even in the funeral home, so he added that the two older sisters disliked their younger sister, and even their mother to some extent, and that he was afraid they wouldn't uphold their end of a verbal agreement he'd made with them.

Before the old man had died, he met with the two older sisters independently and made each of them promise not to enact the will for at least six months after his death, in order to give their younger sibling and mother a chance to get on their feet before they lost their home. He assured me that both had promised they would do as he wished, but then, just a few minutes before I had approached him, he had heard them talking between themselves, and they had said they were going to sell off the home and possessions immediately following the funeral, in order to get their greedy little mitts on the inheritance as soon as possible.

Naturally, this didn't sit well with the old man, whose dying wish had been designed in order to prevent just that from happening. Unfortunately, he hadn't specified this last wish in his will in any way, and so legally, there was nothing that could be done. Even if I told them what his spirit had just said, they would probably laugh it off and not pay any attention. At that point, the old man threatened to haunt them until they kept their promise, but I managed to talk him out of sticking around after the White Light had gone away. The ease with which I talked him out of the haunting was my first clue that the spirit had another card up his sleeve.

"All right," he agreed slyly, smirking at me while his eyes darted over to his bickering granddaughters and seemingly helpless daughter. "Then you do this for me…"

"Okay…"

"You tell my youngest granddaughter to wait for her sisters to go back to their houses, then go into the basement of my house and find the furnace pipe where they hang the laundry to dry. There's a black line on that pipe, and if she grabs it in the middle of the line and twists, it'll come right down, and whatever she finds in there is for her and her mother. They are not to tell the other two about it. They're going to have to do what those two decide—as you say—but what's in that pipe is for my daughter and her youngest. Will you do that?"

"Sure," I said without hesitation—I could see it was the only way to put his spirit at peace, and in just the short time I'd known the family, I knew it was the right thing to do. So I waited until I had the granddaughter who'd called me by herself, then told her exactly what the old man had told me. She was, naturally, shocked and a tad skeptical, but agreed to try it out. It was pretty easy to convince her not to tell the other two sisters, too!

She called me later that night, sounding for all the world like she'd just won the lottery—and in a way, she had. That old man—whether or not he'd anticipated the outcome of his death—had stashed over $30,000 in cash in that pipe—the granddaughter and her mother couldn't have been more thankful.

It ended up that the other two sisters agreed to give them a month to get out. It was something, but it still hadn't been what they'd promised a dying man.

The Secret Drawer

When a priest calls me, it means one of two things: a job he don't want his bishop to find out about or a call on behalf of a parishioner. The latter is usually the case, as it turned out to be on this occasion.

"Mary Ann," the priest said, "I wonder if you could help me. One of my parishioners—a middle-aged woman—just lost her husband quite suddenly. He was the high-powered business type, so of course, he'd had his will all squared away and everything in order such that his wife really isn't placed in a position of need."

"So what can I do?" I wondered. The so-called high-profile business types were not my normal clientele. In fact, that type of person never calls me—ghosts are not real to them, and even if they were, they can't see how to make any money out of it, so what does it matter? Time is money, after all, and time spent talking to little ghosties is just like tossing cash down the toilet.

"Well," the priest said slowly, "his wife didn't really want me to call you, but I pointed out that we had very little choice. You see, all the paperwork is squared away—we're sure of it. We just can't find it anywhere."

"A-ha." I understood now. This guy had provided everything for his wife, like she was just another deal to be made. He'd given her a weekly allowance to run the house, and that was it. She didn't even know how to fill out a check, let alone where to find the checkbook, passbook, insurance papers, or even the will, in the first place! Her kids could have helped her, of course, had they been able to find anything, but the deceased businessman had hidden the important papers very well from burglars—and his family. So here was this widow, living in a huge house, knowing she had lots of money in the bank to run the place, but with absolutely no way of getting to it—her kids were having to loan her money to keep up with her bills. And she didn't even know who her husband's lawyers were!

I told the priest I'd be glad to help her if I could, and the next day, the woman—still nervous and skeptical—called me. I agreed to drive out and meet her, to see if we could sort out her mess.

"There's definitely a male spirit in your house," I told her once I had arrived, describing the man to her.

"That's him," she said decisively, her skepticism melting away, to be replaced by that weirded-out tone of voice. "I knew he'd stick around, to make sure I was OK."

"That's what they usually do!" I added nicely.

"Thank God!" the husband interjected the moment he realized I really could see him and talk to him. "Thank God someone was smart enough to call you!"

"But gee," I laughed back at him, "if you'd been alive, you never would've called someone like me!"

"That's true," he agreed. "I guess I have a different outlook now." He offered me a secretive wink, then got right down to business. "Let's go into the den. Everything's in the desk."

I told the wife this, and she about flipped.

"No it's not! I checked that desk three times! I ripped it apart, and there's nothing there!" Clearly she felt helpless, but she didn't want to appear stupid, too. I felt for her, but that's what her husband was telling me.

"It's a secret drawer," he added once she'd said her piece. "No one could simply find it." That calmed her back down, and we went to the den, where a stately desk stood in the middle of the room, on a small hardwood square surrounded by plush carpeting and massive shelves full of books. If I'd been a burglar, I thought, I would have spent my time searching the shelves for a secret book or two, but he was pointing at the desk.

"Tell her to sit in the chair," he explained, "and feel under the top there for a button."

"Okay…" and I told her. She found the button, no problem.

"Now, the back panel on the top of the desk there," he said, pointing out what looked simply like a paneled design on the desk, "will flip up while she has the button pushed." I told her, and it did.

"Okay, now she can let go of the button, and she needs to pull that little lever under the panel there, until it clicks."

She did.

"Now she needs to punch the button again. Then, while she's holding it in, she needs to push the lever back down and close the panel. I had it made that way so that once the drawer is open, all you have to do is close it if someone comes in, thus keeping it and the mechanism a secret."

I told her, she did it… and nothing happened.

"Nothing happened," the wife stated the obvious; her husband looked perplexed by the fact.

"Push the button," he was mumbling. "Flip the panel, pull the lever... It should've worked. Have her do it all again."

She did, and still nothing happened, even with him going through every detail step by step.

"Okay," he said. "Mary Ann, you get in the chair and try it." I was beginning to get an inkling of why he hadn't trusted her with this before. I followed his instructions, and this time, when I pulled the little lever up I heard a solid click, which I hadn't heard before. She just hadn't pulled hard enough.

"That's it!" he said. When I pushed the button again and closed the flap, a single, file cabinet-sized drawer slid silently out from the right side of the desk. Its seams had been disguised as more fancy paneling.

"How did you...?"

"You really have to yank that lever," I explained.

"Yeah," he agreed. "you won't break it."

The drawer contained all the paperwork she was looking for—most importantly the will and the names of his lawyers. There was also her birthday present hidden away—a pair of the biggest diamond earrings I have ever seen, which, he graciously said, she could go ahead and have early, now that she'd seen them.

We closed the drawer and tried it again with him standing there, and it worked every time. Then we had her try it—really yanking on that lever—and she got it to work, too. I wrote down the instructions for her very carefully—especially the details, like that the panel had to be closed while pushing the lever back down—and she then made three copies of them, so she wouldn't lose the secret. Then she tried it again. And again.

Finally, I got her to go through a tearful goodbye with her husband and made the White Light, which he gladly went into, thanking me again and again for coming out and helping them. Then my job

45

was done, so I got up to leave.

"Mary Ann," she said. "Can we go over the drawer one more time?"

"All right," I sighed. "But it's all written down."

"I know," she said, and led me back into the den, where we tried the drawer again. It worked, just like it should have.

It's funny, though. On the way home, I realized I didn't know where all of the paperwork for Ted and me was "hidden." I knew we didn't have any secret drawers or anything, but still, the second I got back, I had Ted show me. I hadn't run into anything quite like that before. People are strange how they hide things away, and it's easy to see how things get lost when a person dies suddenly. Those kinds of cases don't happen a lot—maybe, every five or six of the funerals I do has little quirks to it like that. For the most part, it's just last good-byes and tying up any loose ends.

Murders

"Hello?" I said into the phone.

"Mary Ann?" a man's voice asked rhetorically. "Detective Bradley. Ready for some psychometry?"

I rolled my eyes and sighed. The police had been calling at an ever-increasing rate, even though I told them over and over again that I was not psychic, that I could help only if I could talk to a spirit.

"John," I replied, trying to sound stern and convincing, "you know I can't do that. My Ability allows me to see and talk to spirits, but it doesn't make me psychic." Psychometry is where a psychic touches an object belonging to a person and can then tell you a variety of things about the person—the police are usually most interested in who the killer is. Sometimes psychics can do the same sort of thing with pictures and through this link can usually lead the investigation down the right path.

"Come on, Mary Ann," he begged, his voice a little more plaintive than usual. "Can't you at least try?" I made the mistake of telling him—once—that very rarely I can get a vibe from a picture or an object. I have since learned that detectives, by their profession, are extremely detail- and order-oriented, and they remember every little thing, neatly tucked away in the appropriate mental file.

I sighed, unwilling—as always—to allow unsolved murders to go unsolved, because that keeps spirits earthbound. Whatever I can do to help, I reckon, is better than doing nothing at all.

"What's the case?" I sighed again, still trying to sound unwilling to cooperate.

"Ahem," he coughed, and I knew right then the short answer was, "It's ugly."

"We have a body, smashed in the face 20 times with a bat, then dumped. It was made to look like a carjacking..." This time he sighed, his brain trying to solve the problem without turning to this last resort.

"We have a suspect in custody," he finally finished. "But no evidence. None. Nothing—"

"I get the idea."

"So, can you come down? Take a look at it?"

"All right," I groaned, standing up. "I'll see what I can do."

Normally the police don't call me so quickly, which only meant that Detective Bradley hadn't been kidding: They clearly had absolutely nothing on the guy, thus he was close to being set free. You can't hold somebody without hard evidence, after all, no matter how certain you are. But the last thing any cop wants is to see a killer run.

I pulled into the station's visitors' lot and grinned to myself, thinking I should have my own spot by now. It wouldn't ever happen, of course, since my type of work, no matter what kind of hard evidence it turns up, is not admissible in Ohio. Everything's really hush-hush, since they don't know whether or not some wily lawyer will get a case thrown out of court the second someone mentions the word "psychic."

Detective Bradley was waiting at the door for me, stamping out a cigarette, when I arrived. He smiled warmly and took me by the elbow when I neared him, opening the door and ushering me through.

"You're my aunt today," he whispered before he opened the main door into the station, and I nodded in understanding. That's how it always is: somebody's aunt or sister or friend, down for a day to visit someone at work. The joke was, everyone at the station knew who I really was, but we all played the game, just in case the infamous courts got wind of something.

We walked straight past the dispatcher with only a cursory nod and knowing grin, then down the short hallway to one of the interrogation rooms.

"Hey, Bill," Detective Bradley said to one of the officers heading out to his cruiser. "This is my aunt, down for a visit."

The policeman smiled and tipped his hat. "Nice to meet you."

"Likewise," I laughed, then followed the detective into the room, where another, younger detective stood expectantly with his arms crossed.

"Detective?" John said. "This is Mary Ann." He shut the door and pulled the blind down. "She's a paranormal investigator."

"Glad to meet you," the young man said, warmly shaking my hand. "Alex Weston. John's told me a lot about you."

"This is his first case like this," John explained absently as he sorted a huge stack of pictures into two different piles. "Figured it'd be best for him to see how things really work." John grinned up at me and added. "Sometimes."

"Right!" I laughed, then turned to the younger detective. "Here I am! Your anonymous tip!"

"Go ahead and fill her in," Detective Bradley asked of his partner. Alex shifted nervously on his feet, so I plopped down in the chair across from John and tried to sound apathetic.

"Go ahead," I declared. "I've heard it all before, I'm sure."

"Right," he agreed, clearly in the odd position of having his senior partner telling him do something he knew he probably—technically—should not be doing.

"Well," he paced, "the car was found out by the tracks on the edge of town. Not such an odd place, really. Lots of people park there, you know, and go for a short hike or…make out, or whatever. Only the driver's seat had a lot of blood and…brain matter on it, which obviously looks pretty suspicious."

"Obviously," I agreed, not liking the sound of the pictures Detective Bradley would soon have me pouring over. And these weren't just little Polaroids: Crime-scene shots are huge 16x16-inch enlargements designed to show all the grisly details. It was not something I enjoyed doing in the least, and even though I knew—and they knew—I could get nothing from the photos, we still had to play the game.

"Her body was found under a bridge nearby, and all her valuables were gone. We suspect it was only made to look like a carjacking and robbery, though. Her husband called and said she was missing—she had two jobs, and something had happened between her going from the one to the other. Well, we got the guy down here for questioning and caught him in enough lies to hold him. What we lack," he concluded, "is the hard, physical evidence."

"I see."

"Okay," John sighed, turning the two stacks of pictures to me. "One stack is the pictures of the body, the other is of the car. Work your magic."

"John, really," I tried to decline, glancing at the first color print of a woman with her face smashed in. "Do we have to do this? You know I can't really—"

"Please," John almost begged, touching my hand. I glanced up at Alex, who was now peering stoically down at me to see what I could do, and I knew, as always, that I least had to produce the facade of doing things the right way. If I got something from the pictures, perhaps the detectives could claim they'd seen it for themselves, which doesn't make a whole lot of sense. I mean, if I see something they can't, it wouldn't be allowed in court anyway, right?

Now, I can do more than one thing at a time—chew gum and walk, if you see what I mean—and since I never enjoy looking at these pictures, I usually think about other things to take my mind off eyes bulging out of a head flattened in by a bat.

"Turns out he stabbed her and strangled her, too," Alex said quietly as I flipped through the stack.

"Nice," I replied. "You'd think one way would be enough."

"That's why we're sure it wasn't a robbery," John expounded. "Thieves kill you and dump you; pissed-off husbands go overboard, if you catch my drift."

"Loud and clear." At this point, I had latched on to her top, and I was thinking how I could never wear anything like it, because I'm too fat, and also that it was clear the body had been dumped by how her legs lay. She was missing a shoe, too, and wearing coveralls, like at least one of her two jobs was in a factory. She was dark-haired, and you could just tell she had been very pretty—at least before her murder. Then I saw that her top was red, with bleach stains up near her left shoulder, and I thought how I would never wear a red top under blue coveralls, even if I could fit into it. Right behind that, though, I realized it was a ruined top—with the bleach stains—and that her job may get it dirtier, so in that case, I probably would wear it, because it was old.

"Boy, that was something about that rain, huh?" Alex suddenly said, thinking out loud.

"Yeah," John agreed emphatically, so I started to really concentrate on the photos, figuring I'd missed something. Her hair was matted down and stringy—mostly from the blood—and the puddles I could see didn't have drops in them, so I was wondering what I'd missed that these two clowns were talking about. The last thing I wanted to do was admit that I hadn't really been looking at the pictures, so I tried to be really cool, burning with curiosity.

"What rain?" I wondered slowly, flipping back a few. "I don't see any rain..."

"There," Alex said, stopping me on the close-up of the bleach stains. "Didn't you see this?"

"Yeah," I said, with a certain guarded relief. "The bleach stains?"

"Oh." Alex glanced at John, who shrugged, then winced and said through his teeth. "Those aren't bleach stains."

"What do you mean!" I shrieked, sure they were using me as the butt of some joke.

"That's a white top," he replied evenly. "The rain splashed on her and washed the blood off those spots—"

"Okay," I declared, slamming my hands down on the table and standing. "That's enough! I can't get anything out of these."

"Are you sure—?"

"Yes, John, I'm sure. Just like I was last time and the time before that."

A thick silence hung in the air for a few moments, the three of us exchanging tight glances and unspoken dares to take it a step further.

"All right," John finally acquiesced, holding up his hands defensively. "Let's go out to the crime scene then, okay?"

Alex looked at me with a questioning expectancy, and I sighed.

"John, I've told you—"

"You told me that sometimes you get a vibe, right?"

"I told you I need to talk to the spirit."

"Well, maybe she's there?" Alex supplied with a shrug; I shook my head slowly.

"No...now why would a spirit hang out where it was killed?"

Alex shrugged again, pulling on evidence from TV and the tabloids.

"There's no one there!" I declared. "They want to hang out where people are, so they can get energy off them and tell someone about what happened."

"Oh," he stood corrected, while John slid back into his coat.

"What about cemeteries?" Alex asked curiously.

"Same thing," I answered as John motioned for us to go out. "Cemeteries are for the living, not the dead. It's where we go to feel better; it gives us peace, because we feel like we're doing something for them. But spirits don't hang out there."

"Well, what do they see?" Alex asked, but John touched his arm and shook his head, putting a finger to his lips as he opened the door. We walked silently down the hall, back out to the parking lot, John saying we were going to lunch as he passed the dispatcher. She winked and nodded, but didn't say anything in return. Once outside and clear of anyone's earshot, Alex picked up his question again.

"What do they see?" he asked. "Aren't they in the spirit world?"

"Not if I can see them," I replied. "If they're haunting a place, it means they're earthbound, which means they see everything just like we do."

Alex opened the front passenger door of John's car and ushered me in as John got behind the wheel, then Alex slid into the backseat, his face still full of questions.

"So if it's just like we see it, does that mean they look all—you know—smashed up, when you see them?"

"No," I said nicely. "The body is what's messed up, not the spirit."

"Is there a spirit world?" he almost mumbled; John glanced at him in the rear view as we headed toward the crime scene, a smirk on his lips since he, too, had once asked all the same questions.

"I don't know," I admitted. "Once they've crossed over into wherever it is—or whatever it is—I can't see them anymore. I'm limited—I can only see earthbound spirits."

"Oh," he decided with disappointment and sat back pensively, watching the city slip past the windows as we headed out of town.

I sat congratulating myself, because usually they sit me in that back room and have me look at those pictures for hours. First one angle, then the next, then close-ups—and I never get anything from them. I think Detective Bradley was worried about his suspect fleeing, though, so he wanted to speed up the process.

"Incidentally..." it suddenly occurred to me; both detectives perked up at my voice, as if I had just sat there and solved the case. "Umm...where did you get the idea that I could do psychometry?"

"Well, remember that case with the nurse?" John said with a shrug; I nodded. "You touched her insulin needle, remember?"

"Yeah..." I agreed slowly, my eyes narrowing.

"Well, then you said you got a vibe from that and that she wasn't really dead, right?"

"Oh yeah," I recalled, cursing myself for admitting to one sudden burst of psychic energy. "But that was a very rare occurrence."

Detective Bradley shrugged again and smirked at me. "We work on rare occurrences all the time."

"I guess," I agreed slowly. By this time, we'd reached the edge of town, and up ahead I could see the train tracks cutting across the road. I shook my head slowly, noticing how out in the middle of nowhere the site was, and wondered how many times it would take me to get through to these detectives that ghosts don't hang out in abandoned areas.

"She's not here," I said with certainty. Alex perked up again, sitting forward.

"How do you know?"

"It's like cheap perfume," I explained. "Ghosts leave a residue. I'm getting nothing."

John glanced at me and smiled, and I knew I hadn't changed his mind. He pulled slowly across the tracks and turned left into a small clearing by the edge of some woods, then cut the engine.

"This is where the car was," he said expectantly.

"Great," I replied apathetically.

"Anything?"

I gave him my best sour look and shook my head.

"You know, we think he did it in front of his little girl," Alex suddenly blurted. I glared at John, who tried to dodge my gaze.

"She has a little girl?" I asked Alex, still glaring at John.

"Yeah, a three-year-old," Alex said with a questioning glance to his partner.

"Well that's where she is!" I said simply. "The mother's spirit will be with her little girl!"

"Let's just check this out, now that we're here, okay?" John asked, opening his door and stepping from the car. I knew that he'd wanted to keep that tidbit from me as long as possible, because he knew what I was going to say, which I did say once I got out of the car.

"Take me to the girl, John!" I demanded plainly. "That's where the spirit is! That's where your answers are!"

"You know I can't do that!" he shot back, walking off ahead of us toward the bridge down the tracks a little way.

I glanced at Alex; he shrugged in agreement with his partner.

"John!" I declared. "Please take me to her daughter! That's where she's going to be!" Most mothers, especially if they have young children, will stay behind to watch over the kids. They think they can help in some way, but soon enough they realize their presence is sapping the child's energy, making it sick all the time and things like that. But a mother who is also a murder victim? There is no way a spirit like that will cross over, and there is only one place she'll hang out.

"We can't do that," he called over his shoulder, his voice almost lost in a stiff wind. "What would they say?" Beside me, Alex trotted to catch up to his partner.

"My guess is they'd say, 'Thank you!'" I called back. "They'd be real happy if this case got solved!"

Alex shot me a look as they stopped and turned back to me. His face said to let it drop, mainly because he felt guilty for having brought up the daughter in the first place. But with each case, you learn something new, and from experience it had become clear that mothers with young kids tended to be with their children. I knew that I didn't have to look at those pictures or waste time waltzing around crime scenes—ghosts want to be near people! Why else would they remain earthbound? Especially murdered spirits—they want someone to know who did it to them, and most times they'll hang out with relatives.

"Mary Ann," John said evenly as I caught up to them, "please do this our way, huh? I'd really hate to get this thing thrown out of court…"

"Fine," I said, throwing up my hands and walking off past them, toward the bridge. What else could I say? I already knew I wasn't going to find anything, but they needed to exhaust every possibility first. So I walked along the tracks, then down the embankment and under the bridge, looking for something I knew I wouldn't find, and these two detectives just kind of walked along behind me, making expectant noises and mumbling to themselves.

In a lot of ways, it is a tremendous responsibility for me. They depend on me for something they can't prove—whatever I tell them, they just have to trust is true. Fortunately, my track record is such that John didn't question me; if I said something, he took my word for it. Of course, it didn't mean the ghost I got the information from wasn't lying. That's never really happened, but it's possible. They could want to get even with someone or frame someone, and so even after death, they'd still feel the same way. Spirits have the exact same personality in death as they did in life. If they were mean-spirited liars alive, chances are, they'll be the same way dead, as well. Although, to be honest, most victims of murder have only one thing in mind: catching the killer. The last thing they're going to do is lie about that, so where the police are concerned, things usually turn out OK.

"Nope," I said stoically, holding my hands up to them in an exaggerated shrug. "She's not here!"

"No vibes?" Alex mumbled, and I wondered if he was beginning to doubt me.

"I don't know what your partner's told you," I said to him, perhaps more scoldingly than I had intended, "but I don't get vibes. I am not psychic. I have to talk to the spirit, which clearly means the person is dead."

"And the spirit isn't here?" Alex checked.

"No, she's not here!" I exclaimed with exasperation. "She...is...with...her...daughter."

"Okay," John agreed, taking me by the elbow. "Let's forget this, all right? We didn't mean to get you upset." He began to lead me back to the car, with Alex in close-pursuit, and something in his voice did manage to calm me down. I guess cops are used to calming people down.

"I'm between a rock and a hard place here, Mary Ann," he admitted quietly. "I don't want to include the family in this if I can help it, just in case a lawyer gets a whiff of psychics solving the case."

I opened my mouth to say something, but he cut me off. "I know you're not psychic, but to the courts you are...you know that."

"Yeah," I sighed heavily. It seems that everyone tells ghost stories—that most gatherings, at some point, turn to good old-fashioned ghost-story telling—but that no one will admit to it in an official sense. So many people have ghostly experiences, but since they don't understand them, they are loath to admit them as fact. It's all purely circumstantial evidence, after all.

"You want to grab a bite to eat?" John wondered as he ushered me back into the passenger seat.

"Sure," I agreed.

Alex scooted into the back and leaned on the bench seat, half-looking at me.

"What's the youngest ghost you've ever seen?" he asked, trying to smooth over his offenses with curiosity.

"Huh?" I asked, snapping out of my own thoughts.

"The youngest ghost," he rephrased. "I mean, you said this lady will be with her kid, right? So who would a kid be with?"

"Oh," I understood, turning slightly to face him as John pulled the car around, back onto the road to town. "I suppose they'd try to be with their parents.

"Actually," I recalled, unaware that his trick to befriend me again had worked. "I can answer both questions with this one case I did— she was the youngest murder victim I've had, and she was looking for her parents."

"Really?" John asked, glancing at me. Like I said, people love ghost stories.

"Yeah—it was this old house that the people were convinced was haunted—"

"Why?" Alex asked.

"Oh, you know, the usual stuff—cable keeps going out, the phones won't work, things moved around or missing, restless sleep, odd dreams—"

"Ghosts can do all that?" Alex wondered with a certain amount of surprise. "By accident, or on purpose?"

"Well, sort of both. Sometimes they'll make the TV go flooky just by standing near it—because they're pure energy—but definitely they can do things on purpose, too, to get your attention."

"Like what?"

"Oh," I sighed. "if you watch TV a lot, they'll mess that up, or the phones if you talk a lot, or they'll hide your car keys or move your stuff around if you're real particular... Whatever they can do to get to you, they'll do it. Unless they're just snooping, then they might—you know—screw up the cable by accident."

"So what about this little girl you came across?" John wondered, trying to get the story back on track.

"Well, they lived in a pretty old house, so at first they just thought the wiring was screwed up. You know, the TV would flicker, and the lights would flicker—that sort of thing. Well, it got so bad that they called an electrician in. He said there was nothing wrong, but they went ahead and had the whole house rewired anyway. But it didn't help. The same things were still happening, so they finally called me."

"How'd they get your name?" Alex cut in.

I shrugged. "Word of mouth—I don't advertise. I mean, I do radio and TV interviews, so a lot of people hear about me that way, but a lot of the time, it's a friend of a friend of a friend who had called me."

Alex nodded; John glanced at me expectantly. I realized then that we'd driven past several fast-food joints and were heading to the other side of town.

"John, where are we going?" I asked slowly.

"I...uhhh....I just want to drive by her house, you know, and see..."

"Is her daughter there?"

"No, she's under her grandparents' custody..."

I rolled my eyes and sighed, but said nothing. "Okay."

"So the girl...?" Alex wondered, steering us out of another disagreement.

"Right... Well, turns out I get there, and there's this four-year-old girl haunting the place. She used to live there, back in the forties. Her parents had shipped her over from Europe to stay with an aunt until the war ended, and they sent money every month to pay for her. Then the parents died—the girl wasn't too clear how—and the money stopped coming, and the aunt—who hadn't really wanted the girl in the first place—decided to get rid of her. So this girl said her aunt would take preserving jars out to the sidewalk in a rag and smash them up, then grind the glass into the girl's sandwiches and force her to eat them."

"What?" John declared with genuine shock—I hadn't thought a homicide detective could be so surprised by a grisly murder. "And she got away with it?"

"It was the forties!" I explained. "Who would've thought this wonderful woman, taking care of her orphaned niece, would be doing something like that? To anyone else, the girl just got really sick and died, right?"

"I guess," John agreed. "But why did she eat the food if she knew it had glass in it?"

"Well, her aunt would stand over her with a belt and force her to—she was four, for God's sake! What else was she going to do?"

John shrugged with acceptance, but said nothing.

"So this little girl hadn't crossed over, because she wanted her mommy and daddy. Actually," I mused out loud, "I've thought about this a lot, because if her parents had really died, this little girl would've seen them in the Light and would've gone to them. So I wonder if the parents hadn't died and were just in a concentration camp, but the aunt had been told they were dead?"

"Yeah—but they would've died in Europe, right?" Alex checked, and I knew what he was getting at.

"Wouldn't make any difference," I explained, shaking my head. "Them being in Europe and her in America? No difference—doesn't matter to spirits."

"Wow," he accepted, sitting back on the seat. "So did you get her to cross over?"

"Sure. I explained that, even if her parents hadn't died then, they probably would have by now, and so they were probably in the Light already."

"That's horrible," John decided as he stopped the car in front of a run-down house. I noticed for the first time that we weren't exactly in the best part of town, and I was glad to be in the company of two armed detectives.

"Anything?" John said without making any move to exit the vehicle. Clearly, we weren't going to be able to go inside, so even if she were there, I didn't know what he wanted me to do. Luckily, I got no sense of her, so I just shook my head slowly, apologetically.

"One last place," he said as he put the car in gear and pulled back onto the road. "Then we'll call this quits, all right?"

"Sure," I agreed and sat back.

"What about lunch?" Alex chirped from the backseat. I was thankful that he had, because my stomach was growling. We'd been wasting time for about two hours already, which meant breakfast had been awhile ago.

"Okay," John gave in. "Where to?"

"Ahh," Alex motioned with apathy, "just hit a drive-through."

After lunch we drove to the impound lot where the car was sitting. Not only was it bloodstained, but the detectives had also ripped it to shreds, looking for clues, so there wasn't much for me to look at. Why they thought a ghost would want to hang around a dumped, blood-splattered, ripped up car I don't know, but we played the little game, and I walked around it, getting nothing but what anyone else could get: a sort of low, sick feeling that this was where someone had lost her life.

"Nope," I said after one circuit of the car. "She's not here. Really," I said firmly. "I need to see her daughter, John, if you want me to help you at all."

"Well…" he winced, scratching the back of his head.

"Where are they from?" I asked pointedly.

"Who?"

"The grandparents."

"I don't know," he shrugged, guessing. "Somewhere in Europe—they have accents."

"John! This is probably a way of life for them! They aren't going to find what I do the least bit strange, I promise you!"

John sighed, then nodded slightly. "Well, let's get you home, and we'll see what we can do." He ushered me back into the car, and I let it drop. He knew what he had to do; I knew what he had to do. Alex even saw what had to be done.

"We'll call you," John said when he pulled up next to my car at the station. "Let you know if anything turns up."

"Talk to them," I almost begged. "I guarantee she's with her daughter."

John nodded. "We'll call you."

*   *   *

Ten days later, I was about to leave the house when the phone rang. I stood in the doorway, looking at it for a few moments, waiting for the receiver to pick itself up and tell me who it was, trying to decide whether or not to let the voicemail kick in. I always answer—

well, most times—when I'm home; having given me this gift, God hardly wants me to ignore those in need.

I dropped my purse and shuffled over to the phone, letting the door swing shut by itself.

"Hello?" I asked cheerfully. Most people that call with ghosts are annoyed or scared or both, so I always try to defuse their mood before they speak.

"Mary Ann—glad we caught you!"

"Detective Weston?" I guessed, not too sure of the voice.

"Yup—your ol' buddy, right?"

"Did you contact the grandmother?" I wondered, cutting right to the chase and no longer trying to hide the fact that he was interrupting.

Alex coughed once, phrasing his reply. "Actually, we did, yes, about 10 minutes ago. She's very anxious—she wants to talk to you."

"Well, gee!" I declared sarcastically. "What a surprise!"

"I gave her this number," he explained, ignoring my sarcasm. "She may be trying to call—I just wanted you to be aware."

"What finally broke you down?" I asked, grinning to myself. It looked like this case would finally get solved.

I could tell Alex had shrugged; there was a grinning defeat in his voice. "What choice did we have, Mary Ann? We have to let this guy go unless we have something more on him than hearsay."

"All right," I acquiesced. "Whatever works!"

"You'll call me as soon as—"

"I'll call you the second anything comes up, yes," I agreed.

"Good," he replied surreptitiously, his voice suddenly veiled. I could hear other voices in the room behind him and understood that someone had come into his office.

"All right, then, Grammy, you take care," he said happily.

I laughed and hung up the phone.

The front door was still open a crack; my dog was nosing at the space, testing the air outside to see if an escape would be worthwhile. Absently, I moved over and scooped him up, pushing the door closed with my foot. I hadn't intended to be gone long, but now that this woman's mother was bound to call, I didn't want to be gone at all. My voicemail usually has 60 or so messages on it—as soon as I listen to a few and erase them, new ones fill it back up—so I didn't want to have to sit through 59 messages to get her name and number; better to just wait. If she was half as eager to solve the case as I would have been, she would have called within—

The phone rang. I dumped the dog and stepped back over, picking it up mid-ring.

"Hello?" I asked cheerfully.

"Is this Mary Ann?" an accented voice asked. Oddly, her voice reminded me of my own grandmother.

"Yes..."

"The policeman called me and said you could help us find my daughter's killer?"

I nodded to myself. "Yes, that's right." I could hear the doubt— not skepticism, but doubt that there would be any help, period—in her voice.

"When can we meet?"

"As soon as possible," I returned. "They have to get this case solved."

"I know," she said, her voice cracking slightly with emotion.

"Is your granddaughter there now?" I asked. Usually I can get an image if there's a spirit present when I'm talking on the phone, but this conversation was coming back blank.

"No, she's at the park with my sister."

"Well, do me a favor," I asked slowly. "When we meet—I won't upset the baby, but you must bring her with you, all right?"

"Yes, of course. The policeman said you thought..." a deep sigh, "You thought Sally would be with her."

"I'm sure of it."

"Can we meet tomorrow?" the grandmother asked, her tone unable to mask her desperation.

"Sure..."

So we set it up for her to come down to my house with the little girl the next morning. I had offered to go there, to keep the family as comfortable as possible, but she declined, saying that she didn't want to ask any more of me than she already had. I'd expected her to be ready for my help, but at the same time she seemed a little too ready, like there was something else. I wondered if maybe she, too, could see spirits on a very limited basis, and so knew that her daughter was there, but was unable to communicate with her.

Promptly at 10 the next morning, their car pulled into the driveway: Two older women and the baby girl. And, of course, the woman's spirit, walking right behind them as they came to the front door.

"Hi!" I said, opening the door to them. They were all expectant smiles and relieved glances. "Come on in!"

"I'm Margaret," the woman I had talked to before said, shaking my hand. "This is my sister, Alicia, and my granddaughter, Janey."

"Very nice to meet you." I ushered them into the front sitting room. The woman's spirit, Sally, kept giving me sidelong gazes, as if trying to figure out whether I really could see her. She was a very beautiful woman: tall, with dark, flowing hair and an enviable figure. The police suspected she'd caught her husband cheating on her, and the only thing I could think was why he'd needed to; surely he hadn't been able to find anyone more attractive? And she didn't strike me as having any sort of bad attitude, apart from the fact that she was annoyed at having been murdered, of course.

"Well," I said, once they'd all taken seats, the mother standing by the sofa nearest her daughter. "Sally is here, too, just as I had suspected." I looked at the spirit and she smiled, relief veritably pouring off her face.

"I'm so glad there's someone to talk to!" she said, and I smiled back at her.

Margaret kind of glanced where I was looking, then looked back at me. "What is she saying?"

"She's very glad to have someone to talk to," I replied, sitting down in a chair diagonal to them. "Most spirits are—that's why they hang around."

"What does she want?" Margaret asked, and I almost asked her back whether that wasn't obvious, but I let Sally answer for herself.

"I want to see my husband pay for his crime," she said stiffly. "And I want to make sure my daughter stays in my mother's hands." I relayed the message, and Margaret nodded sadly, tousling the little girl's hair.

"Yes," she agreed. "His family is suing for custody."

"Oh," I responded sadly. Too often that was the case, and it was the one thing that really kept a lot of spirits earthbound.

What suddenly struck me as odd was that they didn't have any of the usual prove-it-to-me questions. I was really wondering why they believed me so fully, and no matter what I'd told the detectives, it wasn't just because they were European.

"Margaret?" I asked. "I'm curious...why did you call me so quickly?"

She smiled and shuffled in her seat a bit, looking at her granddaughter, then back at me. "Janey's seen her mommy for one thing—isn't that right?"

The girl made agreeable noises, but hadn't really learned to speak yet, other than to say "Mommy" and point at the thin air.

Sally looked pleased as punch, but also a bit frustrated—understandably—and I marveled once again at how perceptive children are. The innocent belief of children is not always a bad thing that adults need to breed out of them; sometimes kids see more and know more than we give them credit for.

"Tell her Mommy loves her," Sally said to me, her eyes puffing up.

"She says she loves you very much, Janey," I relayed. The little girl smiled and glanced over her shoulder, then straightened back up and watched me again.

"But what really got us," Margaret continued, answering my question from before, "is that Sally's brother called us a few days ago. He's a marine," she explained, "so he doesn't get upset about things, but he called kind of panicked, and asked if I knew anyone named Marion or Mary Lynn, and I said no, because I'd never heard the name before. Then he said that he'd been dreaming about his sister and that she was saying this lady—Marion or Mary Lynn—was going to help us, so when the police called with the name Mary Ann, I knew..."

"Oh!" I realized. "Well, there you have it! She got through!" Sally smiled at me with a certain amount of pride, but her face also held a let's-get-on-with-it expression, so I switched from small talk to the real issues at hand.

"Okay," I decided. "Sally? Who did this to you?"

"My husband."

And so the questioning went: me asking, then relaying answers, none of which particularly surprised the two women. It was, in short, very much as they had suspected all along. Sally had been going from her first job as a dental assistant to her second job, working the night shift at some factory or other. She'd gotten off from the dentist's earlier than usual and decided to stop at home to visit Janey before

67

going to the factory. When she arrived, however, she found her husband in bed with not one, but two other women. Needless to say, she became a tad upset at the sight and stormed off to the kitchen, where she found Janey crying in a corner.

She hollered that he'd better get the women out of the house, then turned around to call her mother to come and get Janey while she went to work. As she turned back, her husband ran down the hallway with a stun gun and zapped her, knocking her to the floor, then proceeded to beat her in the face with a bat, all the while with Janey watching and screaming. After several hits to the face, he strangled her—even though she was basically dead already—then he grabbed a steak knife sitting on some dirty dishes and slashed her throat. Overkill, to say the least—and all in front of his daughter.

He grabbed Janey and took her upstairs, then came back down and wrapped Sally up in a shower curtain, took her body into the garage and put her in the trunk of their car. At this point, it became obvious he had been planning this for some time, though not necessarily planning to do it right at that moment, because he moved all of the furniture out of the kitchen and took up the carpeting, replacing it with some used carpet he had bought. His intent, it came out, had been to kill her while she made dinner one night, since he figured the kitchen carpet was the easiest to replace.

After doing that, he cleaned up the splattered blood, moved the furniture back, then drove out to the bridge. Before dumping the body, he actually unwrapped her and sat her in the driver's seat, getting some of the blood and stuff on the seat and wheel to make it look like she'd been beaten there. Then he carried her over and dumped her under the bridge, stole all her valuables, and changed his coveralls and shirt, which he'd bought just for this purpose. He walked to the nearest bar, called his brother, then went home and reported her missing.

"Where's the evidence?" I asked.

"A locker at an abandoned factory," Sally replied. It was no wonder the police hadn't found any evidence: He'd taken the stun gun, the bat, the knife, the carpet, all the clothes he'd worn, and the shower curtain to a locker in an abandoned building and dumped it there, until he could figure out where to put it, once the dust had settled. In literally 10 minutes, I had found out everything the detectives wanted to know: who, how, and where the evidence was. The last question was why.

Sally actually laughed. "For my insurance policy."

"Why is that funny?" I wondered.

"Because he's not the beneficiary," she smirked triumphantly. "Janey is. The money will stay in a trust fund until she's 18."

I had to laugh, too, but I could see she was still upset.

"What's the matter, Sally?" I asked. "We're going to get your husband behind bars."

"I know," she sighed. "But Janey...and the baby."

"Baby?" I asked, then looked to the grandmother and her sister. "Is there another baby?"

"No," Margaret said slowly, shaking her head.

"No," Sally said. "I mean, I was pregnant..."

"Oh my," I replied, passing the news on to Margaret and Alicia. Margaret teared up a bit and wiped her eyes. That's what I hate most about murder cases. I'm not a counselor; all I can tell them is things they need to hear, but don't want to hear, and I never feel very adequate at soothing the pain it causes. When some stranger's house is being haunted by a victim that was murdered 30 years ago, that's one thing—they tell you who did it, then cross over. But this...

"I'm sorry," I tried.

"It's all right..." she lied, Alicia giving her a brief squeeze, though she was getting puffy eyes herself.

"Would you like to cross over now?" I asked Sally. She shook her head.

"No. Not until I see that Janey's safe, with my mother."

"She says she's going to stick around until the custody battle is done," I told them, and they both nodded dourly.

"At least we have a case now," Alicia stated thankfully. "That should make it easier, especially since he did it right in front of—" and she hugged the baby tightly instead of finishing her thought.

"All right," I agreed. "Then I'll tell you how to cross over by yourself, all right? That way you can go whenever you're ready."

"Thank you," the spirit whispered, tearfully joyful.

"Thank you," Margaret unknowingly echoed. "We really appreciate this—does Sally?"

"Oh yes," I assured her. "They always do—just to have someone to tell; to set the record straight. I mean, I just ran into this woman a few days ago who had died in 1974, and she was upset because the cops were going after the wrong person! She just needed to tell someone who'd actually done it."

"Did you manage to help her?" Alicia wondered.

"Well, it turns out the guy she said did it had been arrested for killing someone else, and he was dead now anyway, so it didn't really matter."

"So she...crossed over?"

"Happily. Is there anything else you need?" I checked, since the official business at hand was done. "Sally? Anything else you want them to do?"

"Tell them Janey likes applesauce best, rather than carrots. Or corn, she likes corn, too."

We spent several minutes going over such details, setting things straight, asking any last questions, offering forgiveness, and making tearful amends, until finally we all lapsed into silence. I made sure

Sally knew how to cross over when she was ready—how she could find anyone else's Light, at a funeral home, most likely, and just sneak in that way, since the Light is not specific to any one person—and then I'd done for them all that I could do.

"Call if anything comes up," I told Margaret as I walked them to their car.

"I will...and thank you."

"Anything I can do to help."

The second they'd pulled out of the drive, I hurried back to the house to call Detective Weston, but Sally was still there.

"Sally? What are you doing here?"

"I just wanted to thank you again," she said sincerely.

"It's really my pleasure," I assured her, smiling. "Now go on back to your daughter!"

"Thank you," she said one last time, then vanished.

* * *

"Detective Weston?" I asked.

"Speaking," he acknowledged, not recognizing my voice.

"I'm your anonymous tip concerning the Sally case."

"Ah!" he declared, and I almost thought he'd stuck himself with a straight pin. "Do tell."

So I told him all about the locker, where it was, what he'd find, and how the husband did it. As we spoke, he sent a cruiser and his partner out to find the goods.

The next day, Detective Bradley called me back from his home.

"Just so you know," he said plainly, "we found all the stuff, just like you said, and once we presented all the evidence to him, we gave him the option of not guilty with a capital offense—meaning we would've sought the death penalty—or a guilty plea with a life sentence. He confessed. He's going to be away for a long time."

"Well, that's really good to hear," I admitted. I hadn't been worried about whether or not they'd find the evidence, but then John continued.

"Yeah," he agreed. "The damnedest thing is that, just as we were finishing loading the evidence into the van, the husband's brother turned up. We asked him what he was doing, and he said—with complete innocence—that his brother had asked him to clean the locker out."

"Really?" I asked. "Sally didn't say anything about the brother being involved, other than he gave her husband a ride home."

"I don't know if he was," John sighed. "We definitely don't have enough for a conspiracy charge. Who knows? Maybe he just did whatever his brother asked, without questioning it."

"Maybe," I agreed. "But it just goes to show you…"

"What's that?"

"Next time you'll listen to me sooner. Another 20 minutes and that evidence would've been gone."

"Wouldn't you have been able to ask Sally again, though?"

"Being a ghost doesn't make you psychic," I replied. "If she'd seen him move it, then yes, but I think she's staying pretty close to her daughter now."

"Oh," he concluded thoughtfully. "They don't haunt their murderers?"

"They can," I said. "It just depends on the personality of the ghost. Sally was a regular person, not necessarily vengeful. She's more worried about her daughter than her husband."

"Well, we'll do all we can to help out on that custody thing."

"She'd appreciate that," I agreed.

And they did, too, or else the case was simply cut and dry, because about a year later, Margaret called me back. They'd won custody after a short battle, and Janey doesn't point at the air and say "Mommy" anymore.

Suicides

"My son," the woman said, her voice crackling over the phone. "He was murdered."

"I'm sorry to hear that," I replied sadly. "How can I help you?" The grief was thick in her voice, and I never quiet know what to say to strangers in such situations, even though I know what they want.

"Well, they say it was suicide," she clarified timidly, as if that would cause me to retract my offer to help.

It's an odd thing, but in nearly every suicide I've dealt with, in which a relative of the deceased has called me, the person on the phone is convinced it was actually murder. I suppose it's a way for them to deal with their grief—it's easier to understand murder, in some bizarre way, than it is to understand why someone would take their own life. From what I've found, most suicides are planned events, so you can hardly call them accidents either. Almost every spirit that kills itself stays around. The only exceptions are medical suicides, in which the person wasn't upset or distressed, just worn out and ready to cross over.

But how do you explain to a grieving mother that it was not murder? That her son actually did take his own life?

"They said it was suicide?" I checked, hoping I'd misunderstood her.

"It can't have been," she replied shakily. "Why would he kill himself? He was only 18."

"Well, he's there now," I pointed out. "So I suppose we can ask him."

"That's what I want, yes," the woman sighed. "I want to find out what happened, and I want him to be at peace."

There was an uncomfortable pause; I could tell she wanted to add something, but was unsure exactly how to phrase it.

"But how do you know?" she finally wondered.

"Know what?" I asked soothingly.

"How do you know he's here...now?"

From the sound of it, she'd actually glanced around the room to check for herself; more poignantly for me, I'd seen her do it. If there's a spirit in someone's house and that person calls me, I can see inside the home. As long as the energy is there, I can see in. I don't think the ability is psychic per se, because I am not psychic—at least not in the traditional sense. In an odd way, I think I channel the energy.

When I first started doing this for other people, I lived about 60 miles outside of Cleveland, where I ran a dog grooming shop and took care of foster children, not to mention my own children and aged aunt. Back then, if I got one call every 10 days I thought I was busy, but since they were usually all from Cleveland or that immediate vicinity, I'd wait until I had several cases, then make a day of it. Invariably there were false alarms: people having seen too much TV or too many movies; people who thought their houses were built on an old cemetery; people who jumped at every shadow that moved in every corner of their houses.

I remember clearly this one day I had set aside to go to Cleveland and do three houses. The kids were at school, my aunt was out, and there were no dogs to be groomed, so I bundled up the foster baby and headed to the big city. The three houses were all pretty close together, so there wasn't much driving once I got to the area.

Still, not one of them had any spirits. None. It had been a completely wasted trip, and at this time I still didn't charge anything to cover my expenses!

Well, on the way home I got fouled up in a big traffic jam, and then it began to snow, so my mood just kept getting uglier and uglier. When I finally returned, my aunt tore straight into me for being gone so long, and my kids started giving me hell for not being there when they'd come home from school. A couple of minutes later, when Ted got home from work, I, of course, jumped on him in order to release my own anger at the whole thing.

"That's it!" I said, throwing up my hands in desperation. "I'm not going to do this any more! I'm not appreciated! The dogs like me, so I'll just groom them from now on. If God wants me to do this, He's going to have to think of something else."

Apparently He did want me to continue, because several days later, I discovered my new ability involving phones. By that time, I'd calmed down again, so when the woman called, I didn't get upset and hang up on her, but the whole time she was talking I kept seeing a vase. It was an odd vase—very long, with peacock feathers sticking out of it. The more I saw it, I began to realize it was standing beside a stone fireplace, with pictures of dogs and horses along the mantelpiece. I began to kind of freak out, because I knew I wasn't psychic, yet I had no idea where the image was coming from.

"Can I ask you something?" I finally requested of the lady.

"Sure...what?"

"Do you have a fireplace?"

"Yeah..."

"And does it have a weird vase standing beside it, with peacock feathers in it?"

There was a long pause, then timidly: "Yeah...how do you know that?"

"I don't know," I gasped, feeling chills all over my body. I had a hunch what may be happening, but I don't think I was ready right then, on the phone with this stranger, to fully consider the implications.

"And does your mantelpiece have pictures on it?" I continued, just to be sure. "Of dogs and horses?"

"Yes," the woman whispered. "Oh my God, how do you know that?"

Well, I went to her house as soon as I could, and sure enough, there was a spirit there. And the next time it happened, it was the same. And the next time. And the next. Soon, when someone called, I'd wait for the confirmation of a cross-town peek into their home, and if it didn't come, then I knew the person didn't have any spirits or curses, because there was no energy there for me to channel.

"Are you cleaning closets?" I asked one lady.

"Yes," she replied.

"I thought so, because that's a hell of a pile of clothes on the bed!"

"You can see that?"

And I knew she had a spirit in the house.

Some people have wondered if I'm seeing through the spirits' eyes, but I don't think I am. Nor am I psychic, since this only happens if there is a spirit—or energy from a curse, or what have you—in the home. But it is a response to my request of God, I'd say. It has to be—and it has saved me a lot of time over the years!

"How do you know he's here?" the woman on the phone asked me again, breaking my brief reverie.

"Do you have a white clock hanging on the wall to the left of the sink?"

"Uh-huh," she breathed.

"And you really need to do dishes, don't you?"

"My God," she whispered. "Yes. Please come over and talk to

my son! Tell me who killed him!"

Since she began to cry again, I refrained from telling her, just then, that his own hand had taken his life; that could wait until we were face to face.

* * *

She opened the door holding a bath towel, and for a split second, I thought I'd gotten her out of the shower. Then, as she wiped her eyes, I saw that the towel was what she was using to cry into. Six weeks after her son's death, she was still sobbing so much that she needed a towel to wipe away the tears.

"Come in," she sniffled, opening the door.

"You have a lovely home, Mrs. Horne!" I said, testing the waters.

"Thank you," she mumbled. "But call me Becky."

"All right," I agreed.

"Would you like coffee, Mary Ann?" she asked, wandering down the hallway to the kitchen; I took it as a cue and followed. When I entered, the first thing I saw, with some amusement, was that she'd washed the whole pile of dishes. She smirked at me knowingly and motioned for me to sit at the table.

"Please…make yourself comfortable."

"Thank you."

She was fiddling with the coffeemaker, so I glanced around, and sure enough, there he was, glaring at me from across the room, leaning against the doorway to the dining room. He looked like he had a really bad attitude, and I probably wouldn't have liked him alive, so I knew I wouldn't like him dead.

"Is he here?" Becky asked without turning from the coffeemaker. "I get this feeling he's watching me, you know?"

"Yeah, he's here," I agreed. "And he is watching you."

Becky stopped and turned to me, smiling; I indicated to her where he was, and even though she couldn't see him, she looked at the door and smiled again. "Hi, son. Are you OK?" Then to me. "Can he hear me?"

"Oh yeah," I said. "He can hear and see everything."

"Am I OK?" the young man piped up in a chastising tone of voice. "What the hell does she think? I'm dead, aren't I?"

Well, that proved my feelings about the guy correct, anyway.

"He's all right," I modified for his mother, since my communication with the spirit was silent. "He just wanted to check up on you."

"Who killed him?" she demanded. She wanted to glare at her son, but being unsure if he was still there, she chose to glare at me instead.

"Ha!" he laughed as she sat down beside me at the table, the coffeemaker bubbling and dripping in the corner. "Who killed me? Man, she always was stupid! I killed myself!" he yelled at her, taking a few steps toward us. "What does she think?"

"Becky," I said soothingly, placing my hand on hers. "I'm sorry, but he really did kill himself."

She almost choked on her tears, bringing the towel to her face and burying it in the folds of cloth. Clearly she'd firmly believed he'd been murdered, and now, in one fell swoop, she was forced to accept the truth.

"Who was his last girlfriend?" she asked, her voice muffled through the towel, and I saw that her last-ditch effort was to prove that I was a fraud.

"Well?" I asked the young man, hoping he hadn't caught on. If he was smart, he knew a simple lie here would make his mother kick me out. Fortunately, I think he also saw that I was the only way he had to torture the poor woman further, so he responded truthfully.

79

"My last girlfriend was a slut, Susie, that she didn't like," he replied snidely. "Right, Mom?"

"He says she was named Susie," I said slowly, unable to rephrase it to make it any nicer than it was. "And that she was a slut."

Becky bellowed a fresh wave of tears into the bath towel and nodded vigorously. "That's right! That's right! Oh God! Oh my God! That's right!"

I held her hand firmly, letting her know I was there, and I sincerely started to worry that, if she didn't stop crying soon, she would rupture something and have to go to the hospital. Finally, she lowered the towel and looked at me through red, puffy eyes that seemed more likely to have been the result of a fight than tears.

"Did it hurt?" she wondered. It was the same question almost everyone asks the second they realize it was suicide. Why that's important—more so than with murders—I don't know, but there you have it.

"Of course it hurt!" the lovely young man said. By this time, he was leaning over the table to scream in his mother's face; thankfully, she was unaware. "I slit my wrists, didn't I? Does she think that tickled?"

"He says no," I lied for her sake. "Not much, after the first cut."

"Liar," he accused, glaring at me for a moment. This guy was a real piece of work, all right—as pissed off in death as he was in life, apparently.

"Is he sorry?" she mumbled, and even I knew the answer to that one before the boy replied.

"Sorry?" he gasped incredulously, straightening back up and crossing his arms. "No, I'm not sorry! I'm sorry I didn't do it sooner—"

"Not really," I replied for him, cutting him a stern look. "He says he was very unhappy, but that it wasn't your fault." What else could I say? I couldn't flat out lie, but I could smooth over his harsh responses.

"Why?" she breathed. "What was so bad?"

It was the same question I've been asking myself more and more lately. In the last 10 years, since the late '80s, the rate of teen suicide has increased in direct proportion to the amount the victims' remorse and regret has decreased. I don't understand what is so bad now that so many kids are killing themselves before their lives have begun, and so few of them seem to care. Before, they were mostly sad and upset that they'd actually done it, but not anymore—at least from what I've seen. It's across the board, too—rich, poor, single-parent families. By the time they are 16, 17, 18, these kids have become so disenchanted with life that they commit suicide. In a grisly way, it's fascinating to me. As this young man's mother said, what can be so bad?

"I know you," he suddenly said to me. "I've seen you around...before."

"Really?" I asked curiously. If he was trying to freak me out, it wasn't going to work, and I didn't remember having ever seen him.

"Yeah, at the shops," he said. "You know, where I got my gems and tarot cards and stuff?"

"Oh," I agreed. It was possible. I was in those kinds of shops a lot, what with guest appearances and talks and whatnot, but I still didn't recognize the young man.

"Actually, I think you knew my friend Bobby better," he admitted. At least he was calming down somewhat.

"Yeah? Who's he?" I wondered, now truly curious. Obviously, he wasn't making this up.

"What's he saying?" Becky asked, her eyes darting from me to the space before her where she assumed her son was standing.

"He says he knew me when he was alive."

"Really?" Becky asked incredulously. "How?"

"He used to hang out in metaphysical shops with someone named Bobby—"

Becky nodded slowly. "That's right. I never liked Bobby either."

"Well, at least we agree on something," her son chirped, and for the first time he appeared truly sad. If I was going to get any straight answers from him, this was clearly the route to take.

"Who is this Bobby?" I asked him.

The boy sighed. "This friend of mine—well, I thought he was a friend anyway. I met him once when I was buying some rocks—you know, crystals and stuff—and he told me he was a third-degree wizard and that he'd teach me all he knew—"

"Third-degree wizard?" I cut in. "I've never heard of that. What is it?"

"I think he made it up," the young man sighed. "Anyway, I moved in with him, sort of. He asked his landlord to let me rent the upstairs of the house he lived in, and the landlord said okay. It wasn't a big apartment, but it was home."

"Right," I agreed. Becky looked at me curiously, so I motioned for her to hold on a second, until he was done.

"Well, you know, nothing had gone right. Mom and Dad wanted me to go to Yale—I guess they thought I was a genius or something. I mean, I'd been accepted and all, but I didn't want to do that. I wanted to learn about...this." He opened his arms and motioned around himself. "About the spirit world, I guess. But still, I felt like I'd let them down. They never understood me. Dad was a jerk—he was always yelling at me and telling me how to live and all that. He was so strict—he's really the reason I moved out." He took a moment to glare at his mother, but she was wiping her eyes again and wouldn't have caught it even if she could have seen him.

"So I moved in, and for a couple of weeks, it was great. I was reading a lot about stuff, and Bobby was being really nice—he got high a lot, but that was all right. I just steered clear. And he was always bringing beautiful women home—that's how I met Susie. I didn't know she was a slut until I'd fallen for her." He sighed and rolled his eyes. "Then, this one day, I got home, and me and Bobby were just talking—he was high—and he suddenly started coming on to me, you know? Like trying to kiss me and all, so I got the hell out of there. After that, I couldn't be in the same room with him, and he still hadn't taught me anything."

"So you killed yourself?" I prompted after he lapsed into silence. He shrugged and kind of half-nodded.

"Well, I mean, it wasn't just that, you know? It was everything. I just figured this would be more fun than being alive."

"He figured being dead would be more fun than being alive," I quickly said as an aside to Becky; she nodded slowly. It may not have been the best excuse, but at least she appeared to understand it.

"Is it?" I asked him.

He shook his head, then shrugged again. "You know, I figured I'd haunt Bobby, but he's so high, he can't distinguish between the two. Man, I f-cking hate that guy," he added.

"Why?" I wondered, then added to Becky. "He really didn't like this Bobby guy."

"Oh, Bobby?" she said, her own brow furrowing. "That little creep. Can you believe he actually sent me a bill for cleaning up the apartment—you know, all the blood and stuff?"

"He did what?" her son asked, gaping. I found myself in a similar situation.

"Really?" I checked, shaking my head. Becky's expression said, Believe it or not.

"Let me tell you what else he did," her son said defiantly. "He didn't even call her when I killed myself!"

83

"Who? What do you mean?"

"He left me up there, dead! He heard my body fall off the bed, I guess, and came up. When he saw that I was dead, he stole my box of gems and crystals and my most rare tarot deck, then went back downstairs and pretended like nothing had happened!"

"Oh my," I agreed, shaking my head. I related this part of the story as he told it, all the while Becky's face becoming more and more horror-stricken.

"Yup," her son finished. "He left me there until my mom called to ask where I was, because I hadn't turned up to do laundry. Then he went to see if I was in my room, and he pretended to be all shocked, screaming, 'He's dead! He's dead!' at my mom over the phone."

Clearly, Becky had then called the police and her husband, and the boy's suicide had been discovered, all the while with Bobby successfully passing off his shocked discovery. Becky obviously became upset at the revelation, but there was nothing she could do—or prove, anyway. Fortunately, she called to check up on her son the day after—who knows how long Bobby would have left the body up there otherwise?

Her son was very angry at Bobby for not having called anyone about his suicide, and he was further annoyed that being dead wasn't as much fun as he'd thought. He'd figured he'd be able to throw furniture at Bobby, and when he found out all he could do was mess up the lights and disturb Bobby's sleep, well, he became just as aggravated with death as he had been with life. And he really didn't want Bobby to have any of his stuff.

"Which reminds me," he added, cutting his mom a look that said he was back to his old games. "Tell her to get my CDs back from my cousin."

"He wants his CDs back from his cousin," I told Becky. Her face went white for a moment, as if she hadn't fully believed me until

84

then, but she slowly shook her head in negation.

"Why?" she asked me, then turned to the air before her. "Why, honey? What do you need them for?"

"I just don't want anyone to have my stuff," he declared. "And I don't want my brother to have my clothes."

"Well, what else is she going to do with it?" I asked him plainly.

He shrugged. "I don't know—burn it. I don't want anyone to have my stuff!"

"He doesn't want anyone to have his stuff," I repeated to his mother. She nodded.

"He never did like to share. He got in a big fight once with his brother, because his brother wanted to borrow something, and they ended up breaking a very old vase of mine—ask him who actually broke it."

"Wha—? Okay." So I asked him, and of course he said his brother did, just like when he was alive. I could see this line of investigation wasn't going to get us anywhere, however, so I had Becky tell him she'd get back all of his stuff and then just burn it, and that seemed to calm him back down. I knew that, as soon as he crossed over, it wouldn't matter—she could set up a stand outside and give his stuff away to passersby if she wanted—but until then, it was better to let him think his things would be burned, as he wished.

"Well, are you ready to cross over now?" I asked him after his mother had finished with her last-minute questions about his girl-friends and things of that nature—all the things she'd obviously wanted to ask him, but never had. And, true to form, he didn't give her one straight answer, so she finally gave up and asked, with unhappy exasperation, for me to just get rid of him. She was ready to put her son—and her mind—to rest.

"Yeah," he sighed. "There's nothing going on here."

With a lot of suicides, it's a religious thing. That's why they

85

don't cross over, and I'd guess that 99 percent of suicides do not cross over. Even if they weren't particularly religious in life, there's still that notion in the back of their head that suicide is the biggest mortal sin, and most people don't want to check and see if it's true once they're dead, so they just stay earthbound, rather than risk going to hell.

Especially if they were Catholic, since in Catholicism suicide had long been the most grievous offense. The person didn't get a funeral Mass, didn't get buried in consecrated ground, and went straight to hell. Getting Catholics to cross over is understandably difficult, but thankfully the church has recently rethought its position and now considers those who commit suicide mentally disturbed, thus they can now have funeral Masses and consecrated burials and do not go straight to hell. Once I explain that, most of them are happy to cross over. Some of the spirits have been here for years—like from the Great Depression, when people killed themselves left and right—so their whole families have grown up, their spouses and friends have died, and they have no real reason to stay, other than they're trapped because they can't make the Light.

Becky's son wasn't so worried about religion, but he was kind of having fun hanging out, bugging people in his little ways. Yet, I am a mother, so a lot of the time, talking teenagers into the Light doesn't come from any special abilities—it comes from being a mother. I made it sound like the next big adventure for him. Truthfully, what's beyond the Light is the spirit world, and I have no idea what's there, nor can I talk to spirits once they've crossed over. That was enough to convince him that I was right: Being earthbound is as boring as being alive. For the first time, he smiled at the prospect of something unknown being revealed to him.

"Just one more thing before I go," he said once he saw the Light I'd made for him.

"What's that?" I asked, trying not to sound too anxious. Talking to him had not been any fun, and I couldn't wait to get rid of him.

"If you see Bobby around," he requested. "tell him I know he stole my gems. And even though I know I can't, tell him I'm going to haunt him forever, just to freak him out."

"If I see him, I'll tell him," I agreed, hoping that I would, because that Bobby sounded like such a jerk that I would love to give him a good scare like that.

"And tell Mom bye," he said, then shrugged apathetically. "I guess I am sorry, for her." Then he turned and walked into the Light, and as soon as I couldn't see his back anymore, I closed it up, and we had a done deal.

"He said bye," I told Becky. "And that he was sorry, after all."

"Thank you," Becky said, her eyes dry for the first time since I'd arrived. She half-smiled at me appreciatively, then sighed. "But tell me—he's gone right?"

"Yeah."

"Tell me…was he on drugs?"

I shook my head. "No. Bobby was, but not your son." For whatever reason, most people think those who commit suicide were on drugs, but it's just not true. The church may actually be right for most of them: It probably is due to some mental illness or even just a mild inferiority complex. They figure the world is better off without them; that they're just some big burden. And I think, deep down, that's what Becky's son's problem had been, too. Although I am beginning to wonder if it isn't a fashion thing with teens anymore. It used to be that suicides were a certain type of person—abused or neglected or rejected—and you can almost see why they did it, but now, it's almost like a joyride.

"Do you see a lot of these?" Becky asked timidly, as if reading my mind.

"More than I used to," I admitted.

"You know, my grandfather killed himself," she said. "At first I thought it was him, but then I just knew it was my son."

That is another odd thing: Suicide seems to run in families. I even read somewhere that that's been tested and supposedly proved, and from what I've seen, it's true. It'll just go from generation to generation—one house I did had three ghosts, all from different generations, and all suicides!

"Why did you think it was your grandfather?" I asked.

"Well," she said, smiling a little—it looked good to see her smile. "Actually, there's about five of us—kids and grandkids and his brother—who think we're being haunted by him. But that's not possible, is it?"

"Sure it is," I replied. "He can move from one to the other of you, visiting each for a few days, then moving on. It's odd that he didn't run into your son, but possible, I guess."

"So what can we do to be sure?"

"Get everyone to put a note somewhere obvious that says, 'Bill'—or whatever his name is—'meet me at Becky's house on such-n-such a day at such-n-such a time'—"

"Oh, we couldn't do it here," she said adamantly. "My husband wouldn't like that at all. He doesn't even know about you being here today."

"Oh," I said. "Well, wherever. But then, once you're all there, call me, and we'll see if Grandpa's there as well. If he is, we'll see if we can get him to move on."

"Really?"

"Oh yeah," I said simply. "I do that kind of thing all the time—especially with suicides. They want to keep up on all their relatives."

"You've been so helpful," she said. "How can I thank you enough?"

"I'm just glad to have helped you put your son to rest," I replied truthfully. "It's good to see you both smiling again."

"This has torn us up, you know?" she admitted. "My husband, he went from blaming me to blaming himself to blaming Bobby." She stopped for a second as I stood up to leave, then nodded. "He may not be so far off with that last one."

"From the sounds of it," I agreed, "that was the straw that broke the camel's back. But it's not really anyone's fault, that's what you have to understand."

"Yes," she accepted. "I guess he was trying to find peace...at least now he has."

[Plate 1] Me with Grandma Maria.

[Plate 2] Sometimes ghosts just hang out: The lady standing near the grill (see inset) was not invited to this party.

[Plate 3] Spirits often show up as reflections (see inset).
The spirit attached to this cabinet committed suicide.

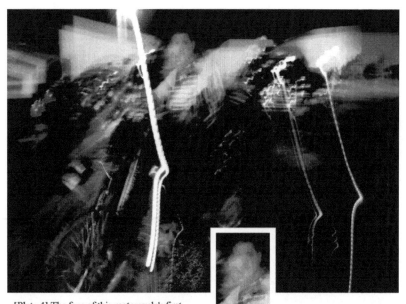

[Plate 4] The face of this motorcycle's first owner, who died on the bike, can clearly be seen in front of the current owner's face (see inset).

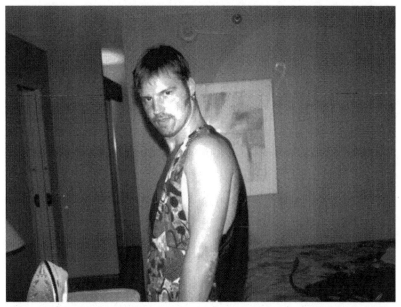

[Plate 5] Spirits often mess with electricity. Notice the "beam" connecting this spirit's "bubble" to the fire alarm, which went off seconds after the picture was taken. Also notice the apparent AIDS ribbon in the bubble: This spirit was attached to a man who leads an alternative lifestyle.

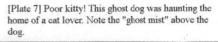

[Plate 6] The thing that threw an ax, trying to hide behind an old car (see inset).

[Plate 7] Poor kitty! This ghost dog was haunting the home of a cat lover. Note the "ghost mist" above the dog.

[Plate 8] This spirit joined a church service. It was not an earthbound entity but some kind of guardian.

[Plate 9] This image appeared on an otherwise clean roll of film, between frames 3A and 3B. The developer denied having processed two negatives at once, and a technical expert corroborated that the image's negative had not been superimposed. (The spirits' faces have been blurred since their identities are not known.)

Accidents

Other than suicides, the hardest group of spirits to convince to cross over is those who suffered accidental deaths. Those spirits are usually pretty angry at having been cut off so quickly and irreversibly. They're angry at God, and sometimes, if the accident was their own fault, they're angry at themselves. And they're frustrated. They want to tie up any loose ends before they move on, but they can't communicate or make themselves known to the living, rendering them powerless. These are people who have consciously decided to not cross over—not out of fear, but out of their ties to the living.

I remember one young man who exemplified this best. I didn't enter the picture until the end of the whole saga, but he quickly filled me in on all the details.

He'd been in a car accident, and the wreck had actually been his fault. He'd not been paying attention and ran a stop sign, killing himself almost instantly as he collided with a truck. At 28—not an age people usually begin thinking about death—he'd had no will or any kind of paperwork in order, but a wife and a two-year-old son had survived him.

He was at his own funeral, of course. That's the point at which the Light opens for a short while, and sure enough, this young man had seen the Light, and had even seen his grandfather inside it, beckoning him to cross over. He'd been very close to his grandfather and was excited to see him and be with him again, but at the same time, he'd been able to see his wife standing beside the casket, crying.

"Why did you die?" she was wailing at his body. "Why did you leave me? You can't leave me! What about your son? What about me? I loved you so much—I'll never love anyone again! How can this happen?" She was just going on and on about her loss, and the sight deeply affected the spirit; he made the decision to stay.

"No!" his grandfather had advised from the White Light. "If you stay, you'll miss your chance to cross over. But if you cross over, you can still come back and visit them."

"How?" the man asked, feeling like his grandfather was telling half-truths merely to convince him to step into the Light.

"In dreams," the old man answered. "We can talk to them in dreams."

But the young man still declined; the tug of his grieving wife was far too strong, and the Light closed up without him, leaving his spirit stuck following his wife around.

She couldn't see him, of course. Their son had no problem seeing and talking to Daddy—as well as a two-year-old can talk, at least. Perhaps if the baby had been able to communicate with his mother better, things would have been different, but all that happened when the child would point at the air and say, "Da-da" was scare his mother. As is so often the case, the child quickly learned not to talk to Daddy or even to see him, and by the time the ordeal had ended—when I was called by the mother some three years later and got the whole story—the five-year-old boy no longer saw spirits.

At the time, however, the father had quickly realized he wasn't able to communicate with his wife and so decided to try entering her dreams, just as his grandfather had alluded. The thing he didn't know was that, once a spirit has crossed over, it is very easy for it to enter dreams, but while earthbound, it is near-impossible. When my Grandma Maria talked to earthbound spirits in her dreams, I don't think they were coming to her as much as she was going out, somehow, to them. I really believe that if she'd have tried, she, too, could have talked to spirits when she was awake, but she liked it being in dreams, so she didn't want to try.

Ghosts know this, too. It's much easier for someone to say, "I dreamed of Grandpa last night, and he said we should go ahead and sell his car," rather than to wake up and see Grandpa sitting on the end of the bed. Spirits know that would scare us terribly, so they come to us in the most unobtrusive way possible. Sometimes, they even warn us. I've been at homes where the person will ask if I can smell roses, for example. I won't be able to, but upon questioning, the person will admit that, yes, it does remind them of a particular person, because she always had roses in the house. A few nights later, they'll dream of that person, and if they heed the warning of the spirit's appearance and prepare themselves, they can—anyone can—actually talk with them in their dreams. The key is that the spirit must have already been in the Light, as if they learn there the things necessary to mingle with the living.

The young man from the car accident had not crossed over, so he was unable to enter his wife's dreams. His inability to do this only frustrated him further. On very, very rare occasions, an earthbound spirit can do it, but it's so rare as to be considered, honestly, impossible, which meant this guy was simply hanging out with his wife and son.

He was a smart guy, and he began to notice that the longer he stayed with her—because he'd go off and visit other relatives, too—the more lethargic she became. She didn't sleep as well with him there, and both she and her son were chronically ill with little colds and the like. It didn't take him long to figure out he was causing the problems—that he was actually like a bad cloud—so he decided to move operations outside until he could contact her. He would look in through the windows and that sort of thing, so as not to adversely affect the family for which he had stayed earthbound.

His wife had been only 25 when he had died. She was young and attractive, in other words, and after about 18 months of moping around, she naturally felt ready to move on, and began dating. As I've said before, people have the same personalities dead as they do alive, and when her husband saw her going out with other men, it made him jealous—especially since she had ranted at him at the funeral, making him choose to stay behind. To be fair, it didn't bother him too much—because he realized that she was young and very much alive—but then, about three years after the wreck, she got married to a new guy, and the spirit's son started calling his stepfather "Daddy."

Now the spirit got pissed.

He could have gone into the Light—he could have been with his grandfather—but he'd stayed for his wife, because she'd said she needed him, and now she'd gone out and found a replacement. Obviously, he was no longer thinking rationally—had he really expected her to never be with another man again for the rest of her life? He became extremely jealous, and recalling what his previous presence in the house had done to her, he moved back inside to make their lives miserable.

His son couldn't see him anymore, but the spirit still went right for the boy, making him sick and giving him earaches and all sorts of minor ailments. He made his wife so moody that the new husband was wondering what the hell he'd got himself into, afraid that her true face was showing, now that they were married. But the new husband was not immune, either, and was suddenly having great difficulty performing in the bedroom—as you would expect as a side-effect to the energy being let off by a tampering dead husband. That further added to the stress, and things kept piling up, and the more stress and energy they expended, the stronger the spirit became.

Luckily, the wife was listening to the radio one day, and she heard me taking listener phone calls and wondered if maybe a ghost was her problem, too.

"Sure enough," I said over the phone. "It's your husband, and he's upset with you."

"Well get rid of him!" she replied, and of course the dead husband was thinking, Oh su now she wants to get rid of me! Before, she wanted me to stay, but now...!

I went over there as soon as I could, on a day when her son would be at school and new husband at work. She didn't want them there, because she didn't want to scare her son or have to explain to her new husband, but she did invite her mother over, which was fortunate for me. As I sat there relaying all of what the spirit told me, the wife sat denying everything, saying she had never said anything like that at funeral.

"Ask her mother," the dead husband told me, so I did.

"Yeah," the mother replied to her daughter. "You were pretty shaken up, and you were saying things like that."

"But I was in shock!" she tried to justify.

"But look at the slimebag she's married to now!" the dead husband shrieked. Suddenly I was the middleman for a domestic dispute. I mean, it wasn't . The new husband was not a slimebag, and the old husband was t angry at her for remarrying, so much as for making him lose his chance to cross over. Finally, I calmed him down, and the mother calmed her daughter down, and we got through the last-minute arrangements that accident victims usually need to clear up before they feel ready to go into the Light. Then I explained to him that, nce he'd crossed over, he could still come back and visit, but that it'd no longer cause any adverse effects, but that by crossing over, would get a lot of answers to his questions. So, I made the White Light, and—tearfully—he did cross over. It was painful for both of them, but at least they got a proper goodbye, which is all anybody really wants, I imagine.

In a way, it was a unique case, because most spouses aren't too concerned with their former partner's love life. Jealousy is natural and does happen—don't get me wrong—but most spirits that die as the result of an accident are more concerned about the insurance money their surviving loved ones should begin receiving.

There was a woman I came across who had been living out by the Chagrin River with her son-in-law and daughter. Those homes butt right up on the river, but the river is at the bottom of a very deep ravine, about 30 or 40 feet down a steep, cliff-like embankment. The woman had moved out there at her daughter's request, because the daughter had been worried. It seems Mom had been depressed, and the daughter thought maybe a change of scenery, and not living alone, would help, so Mom had moved into the house.

One day, she was out walking along the top of the cliff, and she admitted that she had, at one point, looked over and thought how easy it would be to simply kill herself, thereby relieving the burden of her life not only from her own shoulders, but also from her daughter's. No sooner had she thought that than she reeled back from the edge in chilled horror: She had actually, honestly, considered killing herself, and the thought frightened her terribly, because she had no intention of doing anything like that.

Out of fear of losing control—with disastrous results—the woman began to run back to her daughter's house. It was fall, and there were a lot of leaves on the ground, so she didn't see that a tree she was passing had a big root sticking up above the surface of the lawn. Needless to say, she tripped on it, and since she'd been running so close to the edge—because she'd technically been on other people's property and was trying to intrude as little as possible—she had spilled over and tumbled right down the ravine. Her angle and velocity had been such that she kind of bounced down, hitting trees and boulders like a pinba   until she ended up at the bottom of the ravine, right in front of he daughter's property.

When the couple go ome from work that night and found the house open—but no M her—they naturally became worried and went to the edge of the ravine, but the spot where she'd landed couldn't be seen from the op. They spent a sleepless night wondering what had happened en called off work and called the police in the morning to report her missing. The cops said she hadn't been gone long enough to be "missing," but later that day they sent someone out. The detec ve interviewed the couple, and they had to admit that their mother d been depressed, and they had wondered if she'd thrown herself   f the ravine. A search crew was called in, and sure enough, they fo id her body, ruling the death a suicide.

That one little word meant the insurance company voided the policy, and so the bundle of money her mother had thought her daughter would get was suddenly gone. In short, that really ticked Mother off. She began moving things around and slamming doors—anything to really make her presence known. There wasn't much her daughter could do, but when her sister began saying that she'd sensed their mother around and that her kids were saying "Hi, Gamma" to the thin air, they decided to call me and get it straightened out.

Nothing much came of it. They felt better knowing their mother hadn't actually killed herself, but my testimony wasn't going to change the insurance company's mind, so after clearing things up, Mom moved on into th Light and they all put their lives back together.

Only once did my timony change an insurance company's mind, but that was a rare ccasion brought on by a savvy spirit who haunted the right person: I e insurance adjuster.

The story of this spirit's death is rather basic: He had been struck by a train while crossing railroad tracks and had died instantly. He had been on foot, walking over a double-crossing. The first train had passed him, and he'd begun to cross, unaware that there was another train coming from the other direction, since it had been hidden from his view by the first train. He stepped right in front of it—the engineer didn't even see him, but he had heard something and decided to stop the train (which can take a long time), at which point they found the victim's remains. The insurance company ruled the death a suicide, since, they argued, no one can accidentally step in front of a train. The point is, the insurer was trying to get out of paying, and based its decision on a flimsy excuse.

The dead man did not appreciate that.

He'd left behind a wife and two kids who really needed the insurance money. They had talked to the engineer who had been able to convince them—but not the insurance company—that it had not been a suicide, since another train had been passing and had covered the noise and sight of the one that hit the man. Basically, the family was at ease with the man's passing, but the man himself was not.

The first adjuster, who had voided the policy, was not at all receptive. The man had haunted him, but try as he might, he hadn't been able to get to the guy—which may say something about how that adjuster could so heartlessly void the policy in the first place. Awhile passed that way, with the spirit whittling at this stony adjuster, but nothing ever came of it, and the adjuster himself then died. You would think the spirit would stop there, but to him the principle still had not be settled, just moved to someone else.

That someone else was the adjuster who eventually called me. All kinds of things were happening to this guy—chairs moving, things disappearing, windows being broken—but the biggest thing was that all of his electronic stuff kept acting up. The cable TV was out more than it was in. The company even came out and ran whole new lines, and it still went out—but only at this adjuster's house, of course. Lights wouldn't work or kept burning out, to the point that he had the whole house rewired, but even that didn't help. All of this had begun happening after the adjuster was assigned the accidental deaths and suicides policies, and being at least open-minded, he had wondered if the two events weren't connected in some way, so he called me.

Sure enough, it was this guy wanting the decision on his case overturned. Fortunately, the new adjuster was a nice guy, and he agreed to reopen the case. It was tough, but the adjuster got the decision overturned. After that, it was easy to get the spirit to cross over.

With accidents, the spirits are angry and frustrated that they died, and also angry and frustrated that they can't communicate with people to get things cleared up, whether that means their will or setting insurance adjusters straight. You can't blame them for being upset—it's not like a 65 year old man who's seen it coming. When you're young and you get life ripped out from under you—well, I think that would get just about anyone a little bit angry.

Life-Support

"How was the trip?" Ted asked as he greeted me at the airport. I'd been to New York City for a few days, doing various mundane jobs for people who either knew me from the family or had heard of me by word-of-mouth.

"Well, I can tell you I'm not a city person," I sighed. I couldn't wait to get home to my rural setting, sit on the back porch, and sip my coffee. "They had me do a radio spot," I added, and Ted nodded with understanding.

"Start spreadin' the news…" he sang with a grin. "How'd that happen?"

"Well, it turns out Ralph is a big radio honcho up there, so he asked me to do a half-hour spot." I shrugged. "Same as here, really."

"Just more listeners…"

"Don't remind me," I joked. "Someone will probably call as soon as we get home!"

Sometimes, I wish I'd just keep my big mouth shut. No sooner had I plopped my suitcase on the bed than the phone rang. I'm not psychic, but it was one of those times when I just knew it would be a New York call.

"Hello?" I said into the receiver, for once praying it was a sales-man.

"Mary Ann?" a man asked. He sounded at his wits end, but I wasn't picking up any ghostly energies near him…yet.

"Yeah…"

"Hi, my name's Joe Johnson, I'm calling from New York."

"Really?" I asked. Honestly, I was shocked that he was calling from New York, despite what Ted and I had said.

"Yeah—I heard you on the radio this morning. You can get rid of ghosts, right?"

"Yup," I sighed. "And I hate to cut you off, but there's nothing in your house."

There was a pause, and I pictured him glancing around himself, just to be sure. "What?"

"There aren't any ghosts in your house," I explained. "Or wherever you're calling from. Trust me, I can tell."

"I believe you," he stammered. "But that's not exactly why I'm calling. I know my house isn't haunted."

I glanced at the bed, at my still-closed suitcase, and shifted my weight to the other foot, propping the phone against my ear with my shoulder as I rubbed my eyes and tried desperately not to yawn in the man's ear.

"So what can I do for you, Joe?" I wondered.

"Well, I'm one of seven siblings, and my mother is in the hospital on life-support, and we can't decide whether or not to disconnect her—"

"Wait a minute!" I declared, grabbing the phone again and holding my other hand up to the air. "I'm not a therapist, you know!"

"Oh, I know," he agreed hurriedly, but I talked right over him.

"Are you asking me to make that decision for you?" I was flabbergasted; indignant. I couldn't believe the nerve of this man, calling me from New York to ask a total stranger about something that was between his family, his priest, and his doctor. It was absurd! It was the most ludicrous—and somehow offensive—thing I had ever been asked.

"Well, we thought, you know…"

"What a lot of nerve you have calling me!" I cried. "I'm sorry you wasted your call, and I'm sorry you're having problems with this, but there is nothing I can do for you!"

"Yes, but—"

"No!" I shrieked. "Please, talk to your doctor. Call a therapist! There is absolutely nothing I can do! And I'm sorry, but I just got off the plane, so I have to go now."

"I see," he said quietly. "Yes… All right. Thank you."

"Goodbye."

"Bye…"

I felt kind of bad for telling the poor guy off, but I really was taken aback. Why on earth would anyone want a complete stranger telling him what to do with his ailing mother? Most people don't have living wills, and this was a good example as to why, exactly, you should put in legal writ what you do and don't want done, from funeral arrangements to your feelings about being on life-support. It's almost cruel to put your family through that decision when it could have been made earlier, with you present. I realize death is not something people want to think of when they're healthy, but the thing with life-support, especially, is that most people on it are there as the result of something completely unexpected, like a car accident. At the time of his call I had never done a life-support case, and I didn't understand that there was anything I could do. I'd never thought about exactly when the spirit leaves the body—until the day after Joe called, when his doctor called me.

"I want to apologize for Joe's call yesterday," this Dr. Brown said.

"That's all right, I suppose. It really is a decision for you and the family to make."

"Actually," he said slowly. "I have to apologize because I put him up to it."

"What?" I gasped. Was this guy serious? He'd not only had the nerve to think a stranger could help, but he'd then put this poor guy up to calling and getting yelled at by me?

"I really think you can help. What you said on the radio the other day, about spirits in houses and all that? Well, it all makes sense—"

"No!" I cut him off. "Why would you want a total stranger, with no medical background, to make that kind of decision for your patient's family? I thought he had nerve, but you're unbelievable!"

"Now calm down," he begged, and something in his tone at least shut me up. "Let me ask you something."

"What?"

"Have you ever seen someone on life-support?"

At the time, I had not.

"You're very lucky," he admitted. "But don't you think that at some point you will?"

"Yeah," I replied, still in shock. "Someday I'll die, too, but it's not something I dwell on—"

"Hear me out," he asked, then waited for me to stop yelling at him again—I still couldn't believe his nerve! "On life-support, that person is totally dead. If Joe's mother was unplugged, she'd last maybe five minutes, tops. Medically, then, her body is dead. My question is this: If her body is dead, that spirit you talk about, would it be in or out of her body?"

That stumped me. I had no clue, and I had to admit slowly. "I don't know."

"You have no idea?" he repeated. "You've never had any experience with that?"

"I told you I haven't," I answered. Now I was mulling over his question, and he didn't have to ask me to listen.

"Well, you make so much sense with all the other questions about spirits that come up," he said. "Don't you think you should know the answer to this question, too? Aren't you a little bit curious to find out whether she's in her body?"

"Yeah, I guess I am now."

"And if she's not," he concluded, "then don't you think you could ask her whether or not she wants to be on life-support?"

"I see your point..."

"How close is the nearest hospital to you?" he suddenly asked.

"Not far."

"Do they have anyone there on life-support?"

"How would I know?" I asked incredulously. "What do want me to do? Call up information and ask them?"

"Exactly," he replied triumphantly. "You may never get this invitation again, and the Johnson family is willing to pay for your expenses, plus compensation for your time, just to come up here, take a look, and leave."

"Hmmm..." I mused, seeing his point perfectly. He was a pretty smooth talker for a doctor. "If I do it, I literally want to get on a plane, go straight to the hospital, then turn right around and get back on a plane."

"That can be arranged," he answered.

"The driver that picks me up is to go nowhere once he drops me off," I reaffirmed. "I think this is going to be a waste of their money. I'll be in there maybe 10 minutes, then I want to come right back home."

"No problem," he agreed, and the next day I was heading back to New York.

When I got to New York, there was a chauffeur standing at the gate—that was the first time I'd ever arrived at an airport and had someone with my name on a card there to greet me! I'm not sure if it embarrassed or flattered me—then I saw the limo the driver took me to and didn't much care, ether way.

On the way to the hospital, the driver told me he had been instructed to take me out to lunch if I wanted it. Despite the urge to be even more pampered, I declined and asked him to take me straight to the hospital. Ted and I were taking care of many foster children at the time, and the latest—a baby—had just shown up, so the last thing I wanted was to be away from home longer than necessary. Besides, I was extremely curious, to boot!

I knew where I was going in the hospital, since I had finalized plans with Dr. Brown the day before, so after clarifying that the limo driver was not going anywhere, I headed straight up to the correct floor and had the doctor paged. About 5 or 10 minutes later, he showed up—with poor Joe Johnson—and thanked me heartily for agreeing to come.

"No problem," I said, then added to Joe, "And I'm sorry for yelling at you on the phone."

"It's all right," he waved me off politely. "I didn't explain myself very well."

We turned to follow the doctor to the room of Joe's mother, and Joe began to fill me in a bit. "Now let me tell you who all's in the room. There's—"

"Actually, Joe," I said nicely, "it honestly doesn't matter. As I told Dr. Brown, I don't think there's going to be anything for me to see or do. I'll walk in, take a look, and go home."

"All right," he agreed, and we thankfully reached the room before he protested any further.

I turned into the room, and the first thing I noticed was the noise and the smell.

There are so many machines pumping away, and so much disinfectant and what-have-you, that life-support rooms are really almost nauseating, and they really haven't progressed much in the last decade. After seeing those rooms, there's no way I would want to be on life-support, and most of the spirits I've talked to feel the same way. With the exception of people who want to hang on so the family can clear up some business while they're still "alive"—change over bank accounts or clear out safety deposit boxes or the like—most patients want to be unhooked immediately, if not sooner. It's not like there's any rule about a spirit staying with its body until after the funeral, but most of them do. And the White Light stays with them, too, until after the funeral, so they could leave whenever they want to—even if they remain hooked up for 10 years, that White Light will remains until the body is officially dead and buried.

The room of Joe's mother was set up with her bed straight ahead, with most of the equipment on her right, on the other side of the bed. Dotting the room, leaning against the walls or on the window sill or in the few chairs, were the seven siblings and the oldest grandchild, who was 18. There was also the doctor and a nurse...and there she was, standing right next to her body.

"Well, isn't this interesting?" I said to the spirit.

Her face broke into a huge smile. "Oh, thank God you can see me! The kids have been talking and talking about calling you since Dr. Brown brought it up."

"Well, you know why I'm here," I prompted. She smiled with relief.

"Yes. And get me off these lousy things. This is horrible. I want to be disconnected from everything."

Now, you have to remember that our conversation wasn't out loud—they never are with spirits—so to the family's way of think-ing, I'd walked into this room and had proceeded to stop and stare at a blank wall. Finally, Joe asked if she was there, snapping my attention back to the room at large. I said that she was, and, simply put, she did not want to be hooked up to the machines any longer. When I pronounced this, I caught one of the women across the room sort of roll her eyes and shake her head with disbelief. A skeptic.

"That one there," her mother pointed out to me. "The one that rolled her eyes?"

"I saw her," I agreed, talking silently with the spirit again.

"She doesn't believe in any of this," the mother explained. "She didn't want you to come, but when she finally agreed, she said she'd have a question for you to ask me, to test you."

"Okay…"

"Well, her name is Barbara—why don't you tell her the answer before she even asks you?"

"Not a bad idea," I agreed, though I usually have little time for skeptics. If they don't believe, that's their choice, and there's very little I can do about it. "So what's the answer?"

"She wants to know what made up her bouquet for her 16th birthday. Tell her it was 11 white roses and 1 red rose."

"Eleven white and one red?" I double-checked to make sure I got it right; the woman nodded, so I turned to Barbara.

"Barbara?" I began, looking right at her. That alone made her face pale a bit, as she knew I hadn't been introduced and couldn't possibly have been briefed well enough by Joe to fake the names and faces of seven siblings I didn't know from Adam.

"Your mom wants me to tell you something," I continued. She straightened up and kind of fingered her collar nervously, glancing at her relatives as if to discover who had put me up to this. "She wants me to tell you that your 16th birthday bouquet was 11 white roses and 1 red one."

Barbara passed out.

It took the hospital nearly five minutes just to find smelling salts to revive her. But at least I'd passed the test, or so I assumed. So then their mother wanted to give them all a message—a little sentiment that meant something personal to each of them individually.

"If they're all going to pass out, I'm not going to!" I told her. "I don't handle fainting very well."

"They'll be fine," Mom assured me. "Barbara always was a bit of an over-reactor."

"All right," I said to them. "Your mother would like you to know that she does want to be unhooked, but first she would like to tell each of you something..."

I then passed along all the messages, with each one solidifying in their minds that I was the real thing. Even people who say they believe don't always believe—until something like that. When I finished, I asked them if anyone had anything to tell her—can you believe that not one of them did? I think they were still in shock, thinking about their mother's spirit talking to me, but I still found it amazing that not one of them had anything to say to her before she finally died.

It turned out I'd stayed in the room for about a half-hour, but since there was nothing else to do, and I had a plane to catch, I felt it was time for me to leave and let them get on with their business. I made sure their mother knew about the White Light, and that she was going to go into it, then I left the room, followed by the doctor and Joe.

"Well, Dr. Brown," I said. "I guess I'm glad I didn't hang up on you!"

"At least now you know, too," he agreed. "But thank you for humoring me."

"You managed to pique my curiosity."

"Yeah, thanks," Joe added. "It was a tremendous help—I know I'll sleep better."

Of all the ones I've done since, they vary very little—the spirit wants its body unplugged, and the family sleeps more easily. I don't think people realize that once you die, you really don't have any attachment to your body, spirits don't ever want it kept alive just for the sake of keeping the body alive. They see the body as a vessel for the spirit, and they might miss it and might miss being in the world to some degree, but I imagine that feeling of freedom that being pure spirit involves must be more than enough to help people move on, or at least not go back into their bodies. After all, the body is a worldly thing, and the spirit is not—that's why it's such a problem when spirits don't cross over into their world.

The only life-support case I worked on that was any different didn't really illuminate anything more about being on life-support, but rather about what I've always believed happens to very young children who die.

A family had been in a terrible car accident. It had been a snowy night, and a truck had gone left of center, hitting a car. Of the family, the mother died instantly, but the father and six-month-old baby were rushed to the hospital and placed on life-support. The remaining family called me in because they knew I had worked with the police, and apparently there were questions about which vehicle went onto the wrong side of the road, or at least whether their car had crossed the center line.

When I got into the room of the victims and had gotten over the smell and noise, I saw that all three of the spirits were there. The mother was just kind of looking shocked and sad, standing in a corner, while her husband's spirit was in a rage, pacing around the room. He was livid! In fact, his anger was probably the only thing that helped me get him to cross over, because he was so upset at God for killing him and his whole family that he could barely contain his fury. I told him to go into the Light and have it out with God—and as far as I know, he did just that, because he went straight in. After that, it was easy to have his wife follow.

113

Yet the most interesting aspect of the case was that it confirmed for me something I've always told people about babies and very young children: I remember seeing this couple's baby kind of floating in a chair, as if it were being cradled by someone invisible. All I could see was the baby's back and head, and when I went around to the other side, I couldn't see its face, because whoever was holding it was blocking my view—and remember, I can't see spirits that are from the Light, only those that are earthbound.

I went over to the crib to get a look at the baby, but there were so many tubes and machines hooked up to her that I couldn't see anything. I turned back to the chair and walked over, then looked at where I figured the invisible spirit's head would be and asked if I could see the child. Well, wouldn't you know it, the baby was rolled back all nice, bringing her face from the spirit's chest, and I got a good look at the darling little girl. She was so beautiful! I said thank you, and the spirit went back to cradling her. It confirmed for me what I'd always told people about babies' spirits: When a very young child dies, its guardian angel comes back to get it.

Nasty Spirits

When Lucy woke u   a little past three in the morning, and saw the cold eye of a full   on staring at her through the window, her body tensed. She hadn   ven thought about the moon, much less it being full tonight, but n w the weight of realization tied her to her bed, her breath coming n short, expectant gasps. It was always worse with a full moon.

As if on cue, she hea d a knock on the floor out in the hallway. Just one solid rap that   erberated through the small, backwoods home. Her husband had lways blamed the water pipes for such noises, even unconvinci   y going to the basement and banging on a few to prove his point.   experiment had never worked, however. His banging had sounded ike a man on the other side of the house hitting water pipes with wrench; this noise was a slow, methodical knock, as if some creatur   vere requesting entrance.

When Lucy would explain this to him, as she had many times, he'd simply do what he'd lways done when she disagreed with him: He'd backhand her acros   e cheek and tell her to shut up. Memories like that made her gl   , in a way, that he had died a few years ago, but whenever she h   l that knocking, Lucy wished she could bring him back; if noth   else, he'd diverted her attention away from the haunting.

But not back like that ucy corrected herself, squeezing her eyes tightly shut and bringing e covers up just under her nose. Not back from the grave. I don't w it him back like that. She thought through

115

her clarification very clearly, assuming that, if her first, unspoken wish could actually bring her dead husband back, then a more emphatically stated counter-argument would send him back down.

The knock came again, three times in this burst. Slow, menacing raps that had certainly woken Lucy's 23-year-old daughter. Lucy heard movement down the hall; footsteps running toward her room; something pushing open her door.

"Ma?" a scared voice asked. "Ma? You hear it?"

"Yes!" Lucy gasped with relief, sitting up in bed. "Turn the light on, dear."

Her daughter snapped the switch and brought a dull, 25-watt glow to the room. Lucy had never particularly enjoyed bright lights. Once, when she'd been talking to her daughter's psychiatrist, the subject came up, and the doctor had coolly stated that her lighting quirk was due to the abuse of her husband. She had become used to dim lighting, the doctor had explained, because that way the bruises and cuts didn't show up as well. Whatever the real reason, Lucy now wished—as she always did at times like this—that she'd get over it and insert light bulbs that completely obliterated the shadows.

Lucy pulled back the covers and patted the bed beside her, motioning for her daughter to climb in. Her daughter quickly obliged, pulling the covers back around them in a feigned effort to keep warm. Lucy glanced at the window again, at the moon beyond, and thought for the hundredth time that she really should make curtains to pull over the black squares at night. They had no neighbors to worry about, only the shapes that sometimes swirled among the trees.

"Hey, Ma?" Jackie asked quietly as they both sat still, contemplating the silence around them. "Have you seen them?"

"Who, honey?" Lucy asked her daughter, afraid that she knew the answer.

"The...the ghosts," Jackie whispered, as if by saying the word—by admitting to their existence—she would bring them out into the open.

"Hon, did you take your medicine?" Lucy asked, trying to defuse the question. She knew her daughter was slightly unstable—not enough to be under permanent surveillance, but enough that she needed medication, which she rarely took. About once a year, her daughter ended up in a hospital until all her chemicals were in balance again, then she'd be released, and the whole cycle would begin again. The longer it had been since her last hospital stay, the more it seemed she saw the ghosts, and Lucy didn't know if it was due to her daughter's insanity or to the fact that the ghosts preyed on the already-disturbed, since no one would believe them anyway.

"No," Jackie grunted, glancing at the doorway. "But I still saw him."

"Which one?"

There were three more raps on the floor, ending the conversation. The already dim light flickered and faded, then rose back to full power. So far, Lucy thought, nothing too bad. The knocks came again, a bit more urgently and Lucy tensed and shivered despite—or because of—her last thought.

Once, she had seen something, but she'd been tired. She hadn't ever brought it up with Jackie for fear of fueling her daughter's condition, but it nevertheless worried Lucy to think that there was either a real, manifesting entity in their small home, or else she, too, was going slowly mad.

"Did you ever see anything?" Jackie asked, clearly wanting to talk more to keep her mind off the ghosts than because she cared.

"No," Lucy lied, then stopped mid-sentence. She'd been tired, she told herself, but there was that time that she was perched on the edge of the bed, taking her jewelry off and putting it on her nightstand. She turned to swing her feet under the covers, and she glimpsed something—a face out of the corner of her eye. It hadn't been long after her husband died, and she'd been afraid of an intruder, her breath catching in her throat as she turned to face the man. But there was no one there, of course. Just a shadowy corner and the sensation of being watched.

"Maybe," Lucy finally acquiesced, taking the doctor's advice that making Jackie think she was crazy wouldn't help either of them.

"Really?" she breathed, glancing at her mother.

"Out of the corner of my eye—just a glimpse."

"I saw one of them tonight," Jackie admitted firmly, her confidence boosted by her mother's admission.

"You did?"

"Standing outside the window, looking in. A man, dressed like he was from the fifties." As she spoke it, Jackie's breathing became ragged with the memory, and she began to tear up. Lucy hugged her to her chest.

"Oh, honey, it's all right. It wasn't anything—" But Lucy understood that, if it were true, then it meant there was a man walking around outside, looking in their windows. Like moths to a lightbulb, Lucy found her gaze drawn to her own window more frequently, but it only ever revealed the black, moonlit night beyond.

"It was something," Jackie argued solemnly. "And since he disappeared into thin air, I don't think it was a real man."

Lucy's body ran with chills again, and to add to her nerves she heard soft footfalls in the hallway, walking through the house. All of her other children had moved out long ago, many even before her husband had died, to escape not the ghosts, but the abuse. She wondered now how many footsteps she had attributed to one of her kids in the past, and how many of them, like these, had not been made by human feet.

"Hear it?" Jackie hissed; Lucy hugged her more tightly for comfort and protection.

"It's all right," she soothed, trying to sound sure of herself. "They've never hurt us before."

The light flickered again, then went out, and something outside caught Lucy's eye; something white and wispy, like a cloud. Her eyes were drawn to it, and Jackie's gaze soon followed. The two women were huddled together in a darkened room, looking out into the woods beyond, where white, amorphous shapes seemed to dance and spin among the trees.

"Ma..." Jackie said quietly, her voice thick with tears. "You see them, right?"

"I see them, honey," Lucy agreed.

"Make them go away," Jackie whimpered and buried her face under the covers, against her mother's stomach. Lucy ran her fingers through her daughter's hair slowly; thoughtfully. The shapes twisted away through the trees, out of her view, and then the light came back on, and the house returned to silence.

Morning didn't come soon enough for Lucy, but as she opened her eyes on a sunlit world, she couldn't help but smile. No matter what the terrors of the night had been, they were always washed away with the first rays of the sun, as if the ancient superstitions—wrong though they are—were correct, and that ghosts cannot stand the light.

Jackie stirred next to her mother, and her eyes flickered open. Her first, wary glances were furtive and frightened, but once she saw the sun, she also smiled unconsciously and rolled onto her back.

"Doesn't seem like it happened, does it?" Lucy whispered, afraid, to be honest, that such talk would cause the spirits to reappear. The night's events hadn't been the worst they'd ever witnessed, but they had certainly been bad enough. Lucy had encountered much worse in

119

the basement beneath the garage, such that she no longer went anywhere near that part of the house the second the sun began to set. Things had moved in there before. Big things, sometimes, like tool boxes. Her husband had been dead for several years, but so great was her fear of uncovering ghosts that she hadn't even so much as put away the tools he'd been using the day before his heart attack. No, in terms of the whole decade, last night had been nothing.

Jackie stretched and sat up, slipping her legs from the bed and yawning widely. She'd slept restlessly through the last few hours of darkness, but was anxious to get up and do something to take her mind off it; she figured she could always nap later if she was still tired.

Lucy got up as she heard Jackie turn on the water in the shower, her voice singing softly. The sound always soothed Lucy; if nothing else, it meant that her daughter was calm and well-balanced, at least for the time being. There were times when Lucy thought maybe her daughter should be permanently institutionalized, but at the same time, her mother's instinct said that a sterile hospital wasn't what Jackie needed: Her daughter needed a quiet home.

"Hm," Lucy snorted to herself, mumbling. "But it's not quiet here," as she pulled back the covers on the bed and wafted the sheets up and down to straighten them out. As she did it, her body went cold with goosebumps, and she was suddenly afraid. The sheet drifted slowly back to the bed, and Lucy's breath stopped in her throat as she met the cool, not unfriendly gaze of a man standing across from her.

She tried to scream, but only managed to whimper before she backed up and ran into her dresser, knocking ornaments and perfume bottles over, one of which tumbled to the floor and splintered in a cloud of overpowering flowers.

"It's all right," the man said—a fifties-looking man, Lucy realized—but his voice didn't serve to calm her. He seemed to be straining against something, as if trying to fathom the answer to an algebra problem in his head, and his image began to falter.

"Who—?" Lucy finally managed to gasp, but by then, the figure had completely vanished.

Down the hall, she heard her daughter scream.

"Jackie!" Lucy shrieked, her daughter's cry enough to get her moving again. The two women ran into each other in the hall, both pale and shaking.

Jackie began to cry, clutching a towel to her body. "Mom, he was there again. I saw him in the mirror, but when I turned around..."

"I know," Lucy said quietly, hugging her daughter to her chest. "I saw him, too."

"You did?" Jackie asked, her voice muffled by her tears and Lucy's chest.

"Yes," Lucy sighed.

"What are we going to do, Ma?" Jackie wondered, resurfacing and wiping her eyes. "I can't live like this anymore. You know Dad wasn't the only reason the others left."

Lucy nodded solemnly in agreement.

"I saw a lady on TV the other morning," she admitted. "She can get rid of ghosts, I guess. Seemed like a very nice lady—maybe we should call her?"

Jackie's face broke into a brief, relieved smile. "Really?"

"Uh-huh," Lucy agreed, her daughter's reaction giving her strength. It seemed silly now, but the only reason she hadn't called before was that she hadn't wanted Jackie to imagine her mother was crazy. Or maybe she didn't want that woman to come over and tell them there was nothing wrong; that they were both crazy. Fortunately, she'd still written the number down.

"I'll call her right now," Lucy decided and headed to the kitchen with her towel-wrapped daughter in close pursuit.

* * *

"Hello?"

"Hi...uhh...Mary Ann?" Lucy asked slowly.

"Yes, who is this?" I asked.

"My name's Lucy—I saw you on TV last week."

There was a long pause, and Lucy was probably just beginning to wonder if she'd dialed the wrong number when my voice finally came back to her. "Yes, you do have a ghost. Several, actually."

"Oh my God," Lucy gasped, by the sound of it unsure which was more frightening: the fact that she had ghosts or the fact that I knew somehow, without ever having been to her house.

"And tell your daughter to put some clothes on," I added amiably, trying to calm the woman back down.

"How did you—? How could you—?"

For lack of anything concrete to say, Lucy snapped her mouth closed; I chuckled nicely.

"Yeah," I sighed. "I can see you and your daughter standing in your kitchen."

"Go put some clothes on," she whispered to her daughter. Naturally, she began to protest, but I could see Lucy glaring at her until she finally plodded off down the hall to her room.

"How do you do that?" Lucy asked in an almost demanding tone. "Are you psychic?"

"No," I sighed. "But when there is energy in a house, I can see in when we talk on the phone. There's a ghost standing in the dining room behind you and another down the hall watching your daughter get dressed."

"Jackie!" Lucy screamed, holding the phone away from her mouth. "Hurry up, honey, and get back here!" Then, to me, she asked, "How soon can you come out?"

Usually I wait until I have more houses near each other before I take a trip out, but this one was different. There was something decidedly negative in this woman's house—neither of the ghosts in the house at the time, but something else. A lingering presence, almost, that I could sense like an old man's cologne. Of course, I didn't want to further alarm the poor woman—but how could this house be so full of ghosts and such a negative energy?

"I think I better come out today," I finally admitted, without saying more than I had to. "Will you be home?"

"Oh yes," Lucy agreed. Jackie reappeared with a questioning look on her face, and Lucy waved for her to sit at the kitchen table and wait for a moment.

"Tell me, though..." I asked slowly. "I don't mean to pry, but there's an awful lot of energy in your home. Is there a lot of stress between you two?"

"Umm," Lucy began thoughtfully. "There can be. Jackie's schizophrenic."

"Ah," I agreed, then sighed again. "Well, I'll come out after lunch if you tell me how to get there. OK if my husband comes, too? It's his day off."

Lucy paused just long enough for me to ask. "Will your husband be there—would he mind?"

"No," Lucy hastily replied. "He's...my husband died several years ago. It's not him, is it?"

I could hear the slight tremor of fear in Lucy's voice, not needing any kind of special abilities to understand that the woman had been deeply fearful of her husband.

"I don't know, Lucy," I finally admitted. "I don't know what he looked like. The two that were in there before were both younger, maybe in their thirties—"

"Oh no," Lucy decided. "No, Hank was 56 when he died."

"Well, then it wasn't him before."

"But he could be here?"

"He might be," I agreed, not wanting to alarm the poor woman any more. "But we can find out when I'm there, okay?"

"Sure."

* * *

The moment we pulled into the driveway, Ted could feel something amiss.

"Honey," he said to me, "there's something bad here, isn't there?"

"Getting a headache?" I wondered with a casual glance at him. His mouth twitched into a slight smile, and he nodded sheepishly. He wasn't attuned like I was, but sometimes, if the energy was strong enough, he would feel it by physical means—a headache and nausea. Sometimes, he had to wait in the car, away from the house.

"Yeah," he replied.

"Are you going to wait here?"

"Nah," Ted said, trying to pass off his headache as nothing important. "I'd kind of like to see this one, I think."

I chuckled lightly and said, "Okay," as I climbed from the car. Lucy and Jackie were already on the front porch, waiting eagerly, as if we were long-lost relatives.

"Mary Ann?" Lucy called rhetorically.

"Hi...Lucy?" I replied. I glanced around myself at the house, taking it all in. It was a small place, with one floor and a basement, which ran under a two-car garage to the right of the front door. When Lucy motioned for us to enter, we walked into the living room, where a TV blared some talk show or other that Jackie quickly snapped off. Beyond, I could see a kitchen and dining room dividing the back half of the house; a hallway to the left, where dining and living rooms met, led a short way to the bathroom and bed-rooms.

As my eyes roved back around to Lucy and Jackie, I saw, standing in the corner of the dining room watching them, a man who looked to be from the fifties, his hair greased up in a slight pompadour, complete with white T-shirt and jeans, and a pack of cigarettes rolled up in his sleeve. After I'd gazed at him for a few moments, he seemed to realize I could see him, and he shuffled nervously from one foot to the other.

"Do you have any relatives that died when they were about 30—that died in the fifties?" I wondered, trying to sound natural.

Lucy and Jackie exchanged a weak, questioning gaze, then Lucy finally replied after a gulp, "No... you can see the fifties man?"

"Uh-huh," I agreed amiably. "He's in the dining room watching us." All heads turned to see, though none saw the spirit turn and walk off into the kitchen.

"Please," Lucy said. "Sit down—can I get you a drink?"

Ted, Jackie, and I all sat; Ted and I declined the drink without a word, just shaking our heads that it wasn't necessary.

Besides, I thought, I don't want to have to tell her he went into the kitchen.

"So...do you think you can help us?" Jackie blurted, then seemed to think the better of such a pointed, get-on-with-it question. She ducked her head with slight embarrassment and looked away, her face slightly flushed.

"It's OK," I smiled, touching her hand. "Yes, I know I can help you. Right now I see two spirits." I glanced at the hallway to the bed-rooms, where another, older man was standing. Judging by the pictures on the TV stand, this man was not Lucy's husband, either.

"And if that's your husband," I said, pointing at the picture—Lucy nodded that it was—"then neither of them are your husband."

"Fellas?" I said loudly to the spirits. "Come on in here where I can see you."

Like two children who had been caught lighting matches, the spirits both slunk into the opening between living and dining rooms.

"Where'd you get the cigarettes?" I asked jovially as the fifties man lit one up; he stopped mid-puff and considered me for a moment, then simply shrugged secretively.

"Okay," I accepted, adding as an aside to a slightly terrified Jackie and Lucy: "They never tell me where they get their things."

"He's...smoking?" Lucy checked incredulously.

"Oh sure!" I declared. "They smoke, comb their hair, change their clothes—all those things we always do, too. Only I've never been able to figure out where they get the stuff from."

Jackie glanced at her mother and shrugged; if she didn't believe I was talking to ghosts, her attitude appeared to say it didn't really matter.

"So who are they?" Lucy asked, nervously eying the opening where I kept looking.

"Do you know this family?" I asked them; both men shook their heads.

"Then why are you here?"

"It's easy to be here," the older man said.

"How so?"

He shrugged and glanced at his cohort, then said. "There's a lot of energy here."

I nodded; from what little I'd gathered of Lucy's private life, that stood to reason. As if the history of abuse weren't enough, Jackie was also unbalanced, to say the least. Even as they sat there, Lucy's daughter was jiggling and nervously biting her nails, exuding energy for the ghosts to feed off merely by her presence. The more nervous—and unbalanced—she became, the more energy the spirits sapped up.

126

"What are they saying?" Jackie asked. "Why are they here?"

"This house has a lot of energy," I summed up for her. "They like how easy it is for them to be here."

"But there's negative energy," the fifties man suddenly declared. "I'm trying to warn them."

I nodded and glanced around. "I know—I can feel it. When did you fellas die?"

Fifties man shrugged, seemed to calculate, then replied. "1957— I killed myself."

"Oh," I said. "But...why?"

He shrugged again, then produced another cigarette and lit up—I realized that I hadn't seen what had happened to his last smoke.

"Lost my job, and my wife left me," he shrugged again. "It was pretty dumb, I guess, but it's too late now."

"That's true," I agreed. "What about you?"

"I just died," the older man said simply. "Nothing fancy."

"Why didn't you go into the Light?"

He chuckled and looked away. "I saw my grandmother in it—I hated my grandmother."

"Well," I decided. "If I make the Light now, will you two go into it? I can take care of the rest here," I added to the fifties man. He looked unsure, but the older guy shrugged apathetically.

"Can't be worse than this," he said. "Even with grandma."

"I don't know," the fifties man hesitated. "I'm not sure..."

"Look," I said to him. "I don't honestly know what's on the other side of the Light, but if you're worried about it, suicide isn't a sin anymore."

"What?" the fifties man squeaked. "How'd that happen?"

I shrugged. "I don't know—the church just made it that way."

"What are they saying?" Lucy cut in, glancing from the opening to Ted to me.

"Nothing much," I replied absently. "The one killed himself, and the other hates his grandmother, so neither went into the Light before. But I think they're ready to now—right fellas?"

"I guess," the fifties man agreed.

"Nothing worth staying for, really," the older man shrugged.

"All right, then," I said, standing up. "I'll make the White Light on the wall beside you, and you two just walk into it, okay?"

They both nodded, and I concentrated, envisioning the bright White Light that Grandma Maria had shown me. The wall glowed with the circle of radiance, and the two men looked at it with slight grins on their faces; clearly, they hadn't thought there'd be a second chance at this.

"Hey," I said as an afterthought as the two headed for the Light. Both stopped and looked back.

"Thanks for trying to warn them," I said to the fifties man. "If you guys want to come back and see how it turns out, you can—once you've crossed into the Light. You just won't be able to interfere anymore."

Both nodded; the older one glanced at the fifties man and grumbled, "She's still in there," with a glance at the Light. I smirked to myself at what the reunion would be like, but as both men disappeared into the oval, I slowly concentrated and closed it behind them until the room was empty again, save for the living, who were gaping at me expectantly.

"They're gone," I declared simply. "And now I'll have that drink, if you don't mind."

With a relieved smile, Lucy jumped to her feet and moved the party into the kitchen.

"Now," I cautioned as we sat huddled at the kitchen table, steaming hot cups of coffee before us. "It's not quite over yet. I got rid of those two easy enough, but I can tell there are more—what's through there?" I wondered, nodding my head to a door that should logically lead to the garage.

"Oh," Lucy said, her face dropping to worry again. "That's the garage...and basement—"

"I hate the basement, Jackie added. "I'll never go in there."

"No," her mother agreed seriously. "I don't go in there after dark. If the laundry doesn't get done before sunset, it doesn't get done."

"The laundry room's out there?" I wondered, glancing at Ted. The house was very strangely set up, and it had all the appearances of having been greatly reworked since its original floor plan. I had a feeling that what was now a two-car garage had once been the house itself, and that what was now the house had been completely added on at some point.

"Yeah—laundry, garage, basement, well-room..." Lucy added; she glanced at Ted, who had remained pretty quiet the whole time, and asked. "Do you feel anything?"

He nodded dourly. "Yeah. I mean, not like my wife does, but yeah—I know there's something out there." He half-smiled at me, and I stood, prepared to investigate.

"I'm not going in there!" Jackie blurted, her wild eyes switching from her mother to me. She stood, her pent up energy starting to bubble. "I'm not going! You can't make me!" She whimpered and held her head, trotting off into the living room, where she mumbled and spun in a slow circle "I'm not I'm not I'm not I'm not..."

"Honey," Lucy said standing and moving into the living room to hold her daughter. "Hon it's OK. You don't have to—"

"I'll go by myself," I chimed in, trying to help. "I don't mind—"

"No!" Jackie bellowed and tore away from her mother, her body a flurry of activity uncontrolled by her brain. As Ted and I watched, gape-mouthed, the young woman, in a blind rage, literally ran up the dining room wall, like one of those fancy dance steps. When she landed, she plopped straight down and sat on the floor, panting and crying. Lucy ran over and hugged her tightly, saying something we couldn't quite hear.

"Oh yeah," I said under my breath to Ted, "there's a lot of energy in this house."

Ted sighed and raised his eyebrows, nodding in careful agreement. Lucy looked up at us and smiled weakly—apologetically—then helped Jackie to her feet and led her down the hallway to, I assumed, her bedroom. There were more quiet voices, and I barely heard something about them not getting much sleep and that maybe it would be best if Jackie took a nap. Grudgingly, Jackie seemed to agree.

Lucy returned with the same smile on her face, then motioned for us to return to the kitchen.

"Sorry about that—"

"Oh, nonsense," I smiled. "With this many ghosts, I'm surprised you two are as calm as you are!"

"Well..." Lucy agreed politely, knowing full well that most of the problem with her daughter had little to do with ghosts and more to do with the fact that she refused to take her medicine.

"So this is the garage?" I asked, bringing the subject back to the task at hand. I reached out and turned the knob, pushing the door open.

"Yes," Lucy replied needlessly.

"All right," I said with a nod and a reassuring smile, picking up my bag of ghostbusting goodies. "I'll go and check it out." Then I stepped over the threshold and into the garage.

The garage was chilly, but two things struck me immediately: One, the place was a wreck, filled with every notion of junk you could imagine, right down to the rusted-out hulk of a dusty car, which may have been a ghost itself. More importantly, the second thing that struck me was another pair of spirits sitting in that car—passenger and driver, looking at me stoically.

I hadn't even moved from the three steps to the garage floor, and already there were spirits abounding. Yet the thing that disturbed me was not the two fellas in the car—by the looks of them, the older one behind the wheel may have owned the vintage car, while the other looked to be a youth from the seventies—but rather the pervading, so far inexplicable sense of malice the whole place seemed to exude; in the garage itself, that feeling was much greater.

I took the few steps necessary to bring me to the garage floor, and the two spirits watched me expectantly.

"Gentlemen," I sighed; neither spirit flinched. "Okay," I said sarcastically to myself. I was getting the general sense that, while the two spirits seemed harmless enough—bordering on dimwitted, judging by their silent staring—the car itself was far from normal. Not in a Stephen King way, where the car has a mind of its own, but in the good ol' fashioned form of cursed merchandise.

"Lucy!" I called back over my shoulder.

"Yeah?" a nervous reply came back a few seconds later. Clearly no one in the kitchen was making any moves to make the conversation easier.

I sighed again, then hollered my question. "Where'd this car come from?"

"I don't know," Lucy called back thoughtfully. "My husband saw it and dragged it back from a junkyard one day."

"Great..." I decided under my breath. The deceased man of the house couldn't have asked for a curse any more easily.

"Well, he dragged some serious negative energy home, too," I called to Lucy dismally, like a doctor reporting bad news.

"Yeah?"

"Yup..." But something across the way, on the other side of the

131

garage caught my eye. Buried beside a workbench under an opened box of tools—like the garage hadn't been touched since the minute of her husband's death—was a gurney of some kind: big wheels, but more sturdy than a hospital gurney. It rang a faint bell with me.

"Lucy?" I called again.

"Yeah?"

"What the hell is this thing beside the workbench?"

"What thing?"

"Looks like a hospital gurney…?"

"Oh, that. My husband got that at a junkyard, too. It's a casket carrier."

"A what?"

"You know—one of those things they use to wheel caskets around at funerals."

I sighed yet again and shook my head slowly, rolling my eyes. "Oh brother." I took another glance at the men in the car—still watching me silently like I were a giraffe at a drive-in safari park—then walked back up the stairs and into the kitchen, hands on my hips, the small bag of things to help me get rid of ghosts hanging at my side.

"What?" Lucy asked, like a startled child. I leaned against the doorjamb and nodded my head slowly.

"What else did your dear husband drag home? That car has a curse on it, and I'd bet that gurney brought someone into this place."

Lucy shook her head and glanced at Jackie, who had apparently reemerged from her bedroom with our shouting, but she shook her head, too.

"Nothing," Lucy shrugged. "Why, what's out there?"

"Two ghosts," I said. "And a whole lot of negative energy."

"You know," Jackie said quietly, "the last people who lived here were witches."

"Excuse me?" I double-checked, moving into the kitchen; Ted glanced at me apologetically, wishing he could help.

"That's right..." Lucy agreed.

Jackie continued. "Yeah, they had three boys who were all into black magic and all that. Other folks have seen the white clouds dancing outside, and they tell us they'd never seen them before those boys started messing with...you know...things."

"I know," I sighed yet again. "Oh boy."

"Is that bad?" Lucy asked.

"Well, yes," I admitted. "At least, it's not good. Who knows what they called up? You know, it's the darnedest thing," I went on, almost thinking out loud. "Teens seem to get drawn to that sort of black magic and all that—the things these spirits offer them, like power over the girls at school, are very enticing. The problem is, they call these things up, and then they either completely lose control of them or else they tire of them, but can't put them back down. So they call me in."

"Oh," Lucy replied, looking slightly guilty, like it was her own fault. "So...do we need a priest?"

"Nah," I smiled. "I can get rid of them. It's just not any fun."

"What are they?" Jackie wondered. "Demons?"

I didn't feel like setting the woman off again, so I tried to downplay it a bit. "I suppose you can call them that. They're just really negative entities. They aren't of the Light, though—they were never of the Light to begin with." I shrugged again, then half-turned back to the garage, the darkened doorway somehow more sinister now that I had the whole story.

"Careful, hon," Ted said quietly; I gave him a quick, reassuring smile, then stepped back into the garage.

To my right was the car—complete with the two ghosts, which I ignored for the time being—and just beyond it, in the wall on the left, where the two-car bay was divided, was a doorway. I shuffled slowly toward it, feeling the negative energy almost physically, and poked my head around the corner, fully expecting to see the backyard. Actually, I saw the laundry room—really just a wide hallway that did lead to the backyard—with another hallway off to the right.

"Sheesh," I said to myself, wishing I could find the architect and give him a good lashing for such a kooky design. I pushed the door open and stepped into the laundry room, and my eyes lit instantly on the brightest object there: A red-handled ax leaning in the corner beside the backdoor. I sighed and rolled my eyes, shaking my head slowly as I tried to fathom why anyone would leave an ax sitting there in the open like that, just waiting to cut somebody or cause an accident of some kind.

In the hallway, I saw two more doors on the left and right, and at the end a flight of stairs that presumably led down to the basement. I shrugged and stepped into the hallway, stopping at the door on my right. I turned the knob easily and pushed it a short way open— maybe an inch or two—but then it forcibly slammed back shut. The suddenness of the motion surprised me, and I jumped back a step, then went after the door again.

Once more, the knob turned easily, but there was this pressure on the other side, a beating force driving the door closed against me, like a jackhammer was pounding on it from the inside. I changed tactics and tried the door on the left; it glided open easily, but stopped short of opening all the way. The room was small, full of cobwebs and more junk that seemed to swell in the half-shadows and nondescript light, but there were no spirits. Satisfied with that much, I reached in and closed the door again, then turned back to the one on the right.

Still, the jackhammer was pounding on the other side, vibrating up my arm and into my entire frame as I stood there with my hand resting on the knob. There was something in there all right, but whatever it was didn't want to play at that moment, so I left well enough alone and stepped to the end of the hallway to the staircase.

I flipped on the light to the basement and revealed six steps that went to a small landing, then turned back on themselves and went down six more steps into a fully-finished basement. There was an entire family room down there, beneath the garage, going to waste, thanks to the spirits in the house. And I could feel their energy, too. I could feel the residue of the spirits, though I could see none down there now, and I could feel the ever-present sense of gloom that followed me everywhere in the house, like a thick, cloying odor that wouldn't go away. There had been spirits down there—maybe even whatever was pounding behind door number one upstairs. I stopped and listened for a second, but couldn't hear anything, so I turned and went back up, determined to get into that elusive other room.

With a sigh, I stopped in front of the door again, then tentatively reached out and touched it, the knob cool beneath my fingertips. The door was silent; the jackhammer was gone or unwilling to fight anymore. Slowly, I took the knob fully into my hand and turned it, listening intently as the small snick of the catch indicated the door was open. I gave it a slight push in, waiting for the jackhammer to slam it back into my face, but it simply swung silently open, as if nothing had ever been out of the ordinary, revealing a dark hole in the moist ground below.

It was just the well room.

I could feel the latent residue of a recent spiritual inhabitant, but there was nothing to speak of there now. Sure, the well hole gaped in the menacing way any deep hole does, but there was nothing inherently malignant about it. With a sigh, I reached in and grabbed the knob, closing the door once again, then turned and walked back out into the laundry room, still with the pervading sensation of that strong, malignant entity in the air.

I decided to simply get rid of the two idiots in the car, then deal with the elusive nasty entity, so I walked back into the garage with barely a glance at them—still watching me—and put my bag down on the top step to the kitchen, then bent to open it. Very rarely do I find the necessity to take out holy water, but for this case, I decided I could use the extra leverage, just in case. I stepped back toward the car, back toward the laundry room, when I heard a massive swishing noise in the air in front of me. I snapped my attention back to face forward and froze: The red-handled ax was spinning end-over-end right in front of my nose, then it shot off through the air to complete its trajectory, slamming into the garage door to my right. Fortunately, it was an aluminum door, else the ax would have torn right through it. Instead, it made a horrendous crash and bang as it skittered to the floor, then lay there like it had been in that position the entire time.

Timidly, I glanced into the laundry room. The ax was gone all right—it had indeed just flown through the air, spun right before my very nose, and crashed into the garage door with enough force to splinter wood. I backed up a few steps and sat down near my bag.

"What the hell am I doing here?" I asked myself quietly. "This thing threw an ax at me!" I rubbed the tiny vial of holy water thoughtfully, then just as suddenly as the shock had hit me, anger took its place for two reasons: The first was that I knew the nasty entity could not kill me. If it could have, that ax would have planted itself right in my skull. No, that had been a maneuver to try to scare me away, and that got me upset. Though not as upset as the second thought: that the ax could have killed, but had instead slammed— very forcefully and loudly—into the garage door, and no one in the kitchen had even stirred. Not even my husband had called to see if I was still alive!

"I'm OK!" I yelled, releasing my anger at those in the kitchen who still sat silently, but also letting the negative, nasty entity know that there was no way it was going to win this little game.

"All right," Ted called back, and I shook my head slowly.

"That's it," I said to myself and stood up boldly, bringing into view the ugliest entity I've ever seen, hovering right before me on the other side of the car. It was like a skull with indescribable stuff hanging off it—something straight out of a cheesy horror flick, only right there in front of me, in the flesh—so to speak. Its cavernous eyes simply glared, bobbing evilly beside the passenger door; if the spirits inside the car knew it was there, they paid as little attention to it as to everything else.

"You are leaving," I said to the nasty entity with certainty. "You have no choice. You are leaving."

"Make me," the thing gargled maliciously.

"That can be arranged," I provided, full now of my own gusto and anger, channeling my emotions into the one most important mindset I could have: Confidence.

"You two, in the car, you have two choices: You can go into the White Light or you can leave, but you can't stay."

They looked at me, unfazed.

"I'm making the White Light now," I said, concentrating for a moment and putting the man-sized oval on the garage door where the ax had slammed into it. "Are you going to go into it?"

The two men shrugged and nodded, then got slowly out of the vehicle, the nasty entity watching the proceedings with a certain amount of calm curiosity. Slowly, the two shuffled into the Light and disappeared without so much as a glance back, so I turned my attention to the negative skull head before me.

"Now you," I commanded. "Go into the Light. You don't have a choice."

The entity glanced at the oval of light, then shot its cavernous eyes back to me; my confidence had affected the negative spirit, and it was unsure how to proceed.

"Go on," I said again, as if to a bad dog. Slowly, I began to unscrew the cap on my holy water. "This is holy water. I'll use it if I have to. Go back to wherever you came from, but you can't stay here."

Suddenly the thing darted toward the White Light, and before I could react consciously, it disappeared through the garage door beside the oval, which I instinctively closed up around the thin air. It may not have gone into the Light—but then, I suppose it really couldn't have, not ever having been of the Light in the first place—but it was gone from the premises, and at the moment, that was all that mattered. The skull head had mumbled one word before it had vanished, though—or rather, a phrase had been mumbled of which I only caught one word:

"...again..."

I sighed and closed my holy water. What had the phrase been? It could have been anything from Oh no, not again to something as sinister as We will meet again. No matter, really; it was gone from the house. I turned and went back into the kitchen to a mixture of worried and curious faces.

"You okay?" Ted asked, jumping to his feet.

"Fine time to ask me now!" I fired back. "That was an ax that made that noise!"

"Oh God!" Lucy gasped, covering her mouth; both her eyes and Jackie's were wide and afraid.

"Don't worry," I stated dryly, still full of my own energy. "I got rid of everything. It was a nasty little fella, but he's gone now."

Jackie and her mother both sighed heavily.

"Thank you," Lucy said gratefully, standing and coming to my side. "Oh, thank you."

"But you have to get rid of that car," I added simply, pointing into the garage. "It's got negative energy on it, and it may not hurt you directly, but it'll keep you feeling run-down and jumpy, so get rid of it."

"Okay," Lucy agreed.

"I...I still fell weird," Jackie said slowly, almost apologetically.

"They leave residue," I smiled nicely. "It'll go away, now that they're gone. Call me in a few days, let me know."

"What about the cloud forms?" Lucy asked.

I shrugged, producing quince seeds from my bag. "These are special quince seeds that I'll put around the house. Nothing will be able to get in here with the seeds as protection. And once you get rid of that car, put one over the garage doors. I have a feeling the white clouds will move on, now that they don't have anything here to play with."

"Was this the worst case you've ever had?" Jackie asked with a touch of guilt.

"Actually," I replied, "the worst I've ever done involved rats."

"Rats?" the two women wondered.

"Yes," I said, sitting down at the table. The job had taken a lot out of me, and I was ready to just sit for a few moments and catch my breath. "It was this house in a really run-down part of Cleveland. The mother had called me. She had some chronic disease and had an altar set up to the Virgin Mary in her living room."

I caught their glances of incredulity and smiled.

"Yeah—they struck me as the kind of family that ends up in heaps of trouble, then tries to weasel its way out of it, going to extremes to compensate. Not that the disease was her fault," I added, "but you see what I mean?"

"Yeah," Lucy agreed. Everybody's known someone like that, I suppose.

139

"Anyway, this woman's two sons still lived with her. They were both in their forties and wore enough gold around their necks to drown themselves, even though the house was falling apart. They said they had spirits, curses, and everything else.

"Well, they had something, so I went out there. There were several spirits in the house, which were easy enough to get rid of—like your fifties man—but there was another one still in the basement that didn't want to show its face."

"They like basements?" Jackie assumed, with a glance at the garage door.

"Spirits?" I clarified with a shrug. "Not any more than anywhere else. But they're just like people, don't forget, and the basement seems like a good place to hide, right?"

Jackie nodded, so I went on with the tale.

"When I said I had to go into the basement, the two sons looked at each other like I'd just asked them to cut their arms off.

"'Oh my God,' the one said, 'you gotta go downstairs?'

"'That's where it is,' I replied simply. Then the two brothers— these grown men—started hitting each other, arguing about who had to go down with me, just like they were seven-year-olds! 'I'll go by myself,' I finally said, to put an end to it.

"At this point, Mom piped up, 'Oh, you don't want to go down there. We've got really big rats down there.'

"'Rats?' I checked.

"'Yeah,' she repeated. 'Really big ones.'"

"Yikes," Lucy cut in with an exaggerated shudder. "I would've told them to forget it!"

"Well," I agreed, "I would've liked to, but I don't like the thought of leaving spirits earthbound when I can helped them move on.

"Anyway," I continued, judging by their faces that they were

140

enrapt. "I told them I'd be careful and headed for the door, at which point the brothers stopped bickering long enough for one to say, 'I'm not even sure the light down there works.' When I asked for a flashlight, they said they didn't have one, but the same brother offered me his cigarette lighter. I declined and headed for the door again.

"'I'll go,' the same brother said, stepping up behind me, 'But you go first.'

"'Fine,' I agreed and opened the door, at which point a cat leaped out and darted off through the house. It didn't really scare me so much as the two yodles had made me nervous. Apparently they kept the cat locked down there to kill the rats, but judging by the poor animal's size, two rats could've beaten it up!"

"That's cruel," Jackie mumbled. I shrugged—that was the type of people I'd been dealing with.

"So, I go down the stairs and see that there is just junk everywhere—boxes piled high and all sorts of stuff. There was a small walkway threaded through the junk to my right, and at the end of it was a door with a target painted on it. At this point, the string from the light hit me in the face, so I yanked it and lit up the place, and the first thing I saw is that the target on the door has bullet holes around it."

"Bullet holes?" Lucy checked; Ted just sat and grinned at all of their reactions. He'd heard me tell the story a hundred times, always with similar responses.

"Yup," I continued. "Bullet holes. They used to practice with a . 38 in the basement, shooting at the door! Anyway, I could tell that whatever spirit was there was behind the door, and I half-wondered with a prickle on my neck if it wasn't someone they'd shot back there for target practice. Regardless, I figured it was too late now, so I headed straight for the slatted wooden door.

"'Don't open that,' the brother said from his vantage point on the stairs, peeking down at me. Suddenly, I seriously considered my fears of a dead body with a pissed-off spirit.

"'Why not?' I wondered curiously, glancing back at him. He shrugged.

"'I don't know—we haven't opened it in about 20 years.'

"'Well,' I replied and turned back to the door, grabbing its rusty handle and giving it a good yank, 'this is where the ghost is.' I glanced back and saw that my fearless escort had already backed up a few steps. Turning back to the door, I couldn't see anything, so I decided to take a quick peek inside. I had just stuck my head in when something hit me and scratched the base of my neck.

"I shrieked, of course, and jumped back, at which point I heard the brother yell, 'Oh my God! A rat jumped on you!' I moved my hand away from my neck, revealing a deep scratch that was bleeding. 'Look at the blood!' he screamed and bolted back up the stairs, slamming the door behind him!"

"Oh, a rat," Lucy said sagely. "That could've been nasty."

"Yes," I agreed, "except it hadn't been a rat. It was the spirit that did that to me."

"Oh my goodness," she gasped, covering her mouth; Jackie gaped, too, and Ted just shrugged as if to say, Strange but true, I'm afraid.

"Needless to say, I quickly learned not to stick my head into dark doorways until I'm sure there's nothing there."

"I'll say," Lucy agreed.

"So anyway," I finished, "I was angry at the ghost for scratching me and angry at the brother for belting out of there, so I just turned and kind of got rid of the ghost without thinking. I just made the Light, ordered it in, and closed it up behind it. Then I headed back upstairs. At first I thought the brother was leaning against the door or had locked me in, and my fears were suddenly renewed. After all, I'd not had time to ask the nasty little ghost why it was there, so it could still have been a murder victim. But a firm push quelled my fears as the door sprung open.

"I went straight to the sink and cleaned up the cut as best I could, then noticed that the family had retreated to the dining room when numbskull had bolted from the basement. I stepped in to tell them what had happened, and the mother just in shock.

"'Oh—you better get rabies shot,' she said.

"'That wasn't a rat,' I replied calmly, 'That was the spirit that did this!'

"'Huh?' the brothers said in unison, and the mother added, 'Is it gone?'

"'Yeah, it's gone,' I replied, and as soon as possible, I was gone, too!"

"Wow," Jackie breathed. "Do many of them draw blood?"

"Not really," I answered. "Not as long as I remain alert to them, which is hard to do in a dark, rat-infested basement. As soon as I let my guard down or poke my head in where I shouldn't, something like that happens. Usually just a scratch. Sometimes they bleed, but no permanent scars or anything."

"Can I get you a coffee?" Lucy suddenly asked, remembering her manners with a guilty look.

"Oh, no, that's OK," I said. "We'd better get going."

Ted and I stood up and wandered toward the front door, the two women behind us.

"All right," Lucy said. "Thank you so much!"

"My pleasure," I smiled. "Call me in a week or so and let me know how the house feels. And get rid of that car!"

"I will," Lucy agreed to both requests.

* * *

A week later, the phone rang. It was Lucy, checking in with me.

"There's nothing there now," I said happily.

"Really?" Lucy checked, sounding refreshed and alive.

"Sure. I can't see into your home this time, so I know it's clean—of spirits, anyway!"

Lucy chuckled. "Yeah—but I still have some dishes to do!"

"So how's the house feel?"

"Great," Lucy sighed. "It seems sunnier and brighter, and the air seems less dense somehow."

"Well, that's what getting rid of those things will do for you! So I guess you took care of the car?"

"Yeah," Lucy admitted with a slightly guilty tone. "We couldn't afford to pay someone to tow it, but a friend of mine, her husband has a tow truck, so he just took it and dumped it for us."

"Good," I replied thankfully. "But why do you sound so...sad about it?"

"Oh—I'm not sad about getting rid of it, but her husband...?"

"Yeah...?"

"Well, he just took it and dumped it over a ravine back here like most folks do, but as he did it, something weird happened."

"What?" I wondered, fearing another trip to the sticks to ferret out more nasties in another garage.

"Well, there was a freak accident. Her husband has never seen anything like it before, in all his days of towing and dumping things. One of the hooks, when he was releasing the car over the edge, somehow snapped back and caught him right under the knee. Smashed his leg so bad..." Lucy sighed, holding back guilty tears. "...Smashed it so badly he had to have it removed below the knee."

"My goodness," I breathed, not at all surprised, to be honest. "See? And that car was sitting in your garage all those years, fueling that negative entity!"

"Yeah...I'm just so it happened, you know? He was helping us out 'n' all..."

"Did he know the whole story?" I asked.

"Yeah—that's why he agreed to do it. Says he doesn't hold anything against us, but still..."

"I know," I agreed, sympathizing with her.

Animals

Sam

I don't remember ever seeing animal spirits before it was brought to my attention by a little boy. He'd died in the 1930s, the result of a fire that killed his whole family. It turned out that the little boy had been responsible for the fire, and I found out the hard way that the last person he wanted to see in the Light was his father. Or his mother or grandmother, who'd also died. That's right about when I learned that you ask a spirit who it wants to see in the Light, then tell it that person is there. I'd hate to say I'm lying, but my main objective is to get the spirit into that Light.

So, after learning how he'd died and all that, I was at a loss—how was I going to talk him into the Light, now that he knew he'd see his father? At wits' end, I asked the little guy who he did want to see again, hoping I could recover from my previous assumption.

"Sam," he said.

"Sam? Was he your brother?"

"No," the kid said in that typical, pouty kid fashion. "Sam was my dog."

"Oh."

Having never considered that animals might have earthbound spirits, I honestly didn't know what to say. But I could tell that he really wanted to see that dog, so I bluffed and replied, "Well, sure he'll be in there!"

"Lady, are you telling me the truth?"

"Of course I am!" I pronounced, trying to think if there was any reason animals shouldn't cross over as humans do. I made the White Light for him to go into and he took a few slow steps toward it. Actually, "slow" doesn't come close to describing his shuffle—he must really have been afraid of meeting up with his family again, and he barely moved his feet in the direction of the White Light. I was getting kind of antsy, mainly because I had no idea what to do if he called my bluff and refused to enter the Light. After a few shuffles, he stopped and turned slowly around to me.

His face was nothing but a huge grin.

"I see Sam!" he breathed. "Thanks, Lady!" Then he broke into a run and dashed into the Light. If nothing else, the experience confirmed in my mind that animals do cross over.

Since then I have seen all kinds of animals, but mostly what I would think of as the higher intelligences: I've seen dogs, cats, deer, elk, moose, wolves, foxes, and hawks, and I even saw my hedgehog for a few days after it died. None of the animals I've seen seem particularly upset or skittish—in fact, they seem a tad more social, if anything. I don't know, maybe there are little elves or gnomes that usually help them cross over, or maybe it's instinct, but either way, enough of them stay to keep me busy! Cats are the worst animal spirits, to be honest. They usually only cause problems for other cats, but I cannot get them to cross over. They're very stubborn, and I have to try to find an earthbound spirit who's ready to cross over and will take the cat with it!

I've found that animals are just like people—if they were mean in life, they're still grumpy in death. Pets usually manage to follow their owners, but sometimes they get left behind. The biggest difference is getting them through the Light, since I can't reason with them and sweet-talk them through. The one thing I'm not really sure about is where they go when they cross over. Logic dictates that the little boy, with his dog Sam, proved that they go where everyone goes, and I suppose that makes a certain amount of sense—I've let murderers, rapists, and sweet old men into that Light, so why not dogs and cats?

An Odd Pet

Perhaps the strangest animal I've dealt with was in a lady's one-bedroom apartment. She'd called and said that, whenever she went to sleep, she felt like her arms and legs were tied down and that there was something lying across her throat. And every morning, she'd make her bed all nice and neat, but when she got home from work, it'd be messed up with what she called "tunnels," which she described as really big wrinkles in the thick bedding.

When she called me to talk about it, I could sense an earthbound energy, but I couldn't tell what it was—I knew it wasn't a person, at least. That kind of set me up to be freaked out, because I've never liked the "other" entities that are usually the result of somebody dabbling in witchcraft or whatever you want to call it, and with this woman saying it pinned her to the bed and put pressure on her throat...well, it didn't conjure a good image.

She lived alone in a three-room place. As soon as I stepped inside I could feel the entity, but I still couldn't figure out what it was.

"It's in there," I said, pointing to her bedroom.

"Well, that's the bedroom," she said. "And look at the bedding! I didn't remake it this afternoon." It was just as she'd said over the phone: huge wrinkles that looked like tunnels, as if something had been burrowing under the covers.

"It's in the closet no ' I said. "Do you mind if I take a peek?"

"Not at all," she repl d hastily.

I went over and turn : the knob, never liking the game-show-like aspect of finding out what was behind door number one, and it was that sense of the entirely unknown that got to me. The woman was standing by the door, ready to bolt, I imagine, which didn't do much to settle my nerves. I slowly swung open that door—ready, quite frankly, to bolt myself, if need be.

I took one quick peek and didn't see anything at first, but then my eyes went to the floor, where a few blankets were piled, and I slammed the door and scooted quickly back across the room.

"What?" the woman gasped.

"Oh...my...God," I breathed, trying to slow my heart rate.

"What?" she pleaded, naturally a bit worried. "What is it?"

"A snake."

"A snake?" she shrieked.

"Yup," I nodded. "A big boa, all curled up in the corner."

"I've been sleeping with a snake in the bed?" She was almost hysterical, but I don't think she realized how much I can't stand snakes. I don't even do earthworms, let alone boa constrictors.

"You have to get rid of it," she demanded. I gaped at her.

"Well, how?" I asked. more of myself than her. "I can't exactly call it and tell it to cross over."

"I don't know," she shuddered, glancing at the tunnels all over her bed. "But you've got to do something."

I thought for a moment, and then it occurred to me that I usually made the White Light on a wall, but there was no reason I couldn't make it on the floor, right under the snake. And in theory, the snake should then just fall right through.

"Okay," I sighed. "I have an idea." I took in a deep breath, then shuffled back over to the closet door. It was stupid to feel safe with the door closed, because I knew spirits could walk right through them, and I assume snakes would be no different. But still, the slowness with which I opened that door was equaled only by the speed with which I made the White Light on the floor, watched the boa drop right in, then shut the oval again. And let out my breath in a huge sigh.

"It's gone."

"Gone?"

"Yeah, he dropped right in." All 10 feet of it, it turned out. The woman called me later and said that she'd found out the previous occupant had owned a huge boa that died right before he moved out. My experience since then has been that a pet's spirit will follow its owner, but then, I suppose snakes can't crawl too far—and that guy had moved to Texas.

Little Major

My own pet followed us when we moved. He was a little Bichon Frise, a rare breed that looks like a small poodle, only with a long tail. I'd had him since he was six and a half months old—little Major was definitely my dog. He followed me everywhere. He was a really good little guy, except that he wasn't allowed up on the furniture, but when I'd come home, the pillows would be on the floor anyway, and you could see a depression in the afghan where he'd curled up his little body. Well, it was like a game to him, just like the way he'd climb up on the bed whenever I was trying to make it. So just about every day, I'd come home, the pillows would be on the floor, and I'd yell at him, and his little ears would flatten down, and he'd slink away.

He was allowed on the bed, and he'd curl up either between Ted and I at our feet, or between Ted's legs. Even though he was only 10 pounds, the weight still put Ted's legs to sleep if Major stayed there long enough, and Ted got in the habit of "scissoring" him—he'd bring his legs together until Major got the hint and moved.

We'd had Major about 17 years when he died—we had to have him put to sleep—and I didn't see him for the longest time, but then, I wasn't really looking. Then one day, I remember coming home, and the pillows from the couch were on the floor, just like when major had been alive. I took a quick look around for him, but couldn't find him, so I didn't think too much about it. Soon after that, I was talking on the phone, and I'd gotten into the habit of sitting at the same place while I talked on the phone, and Major would always curl up at my feet, so I got used to checking for him whenever I moved. Well, after 17 years, it becomes more than habit, and I just looked down without thinking, and lo and behold, Major was curled up at my feet!

"Major!" I said, and he looked up at me and wagged his little tail, just as though he were still alive. Well, I made the White Light right then and there, and told Major to go into it, but he just stood and looked at me with his ears flattened down like I was yelling at him.

So I said, "Fine, you don't have to go—but stay off the couch!" and he slunk away like he always did. Major's still with us to this day. Some days Ted will wake up and say, "Major slept with us last night," and I'll still come home and find the couch pillows on the floor.

When we moved, I really didn't think Major would follow us. When I had my grooming shop I always told people that, if a dog died, never get the same breed, because you just end up comparing it to the first dog. Of course, I didn't follow my own advice, and once we were settled into the new house, I got another Bichon Frise— which is how I found out that Major had followed us.

He drove that puppy crazy! It wouldn't do anything we told it—it'd sit and potty on the floor right in front of me, as I watched it. It never listened and just could not be trained, so we finally got rid of it. Of course, the new owners never had any trouble at all—they even thanked me for house-training it so well. I haven't brought another puppy into the house since then, because I know Major's with us and that he'd torture any new dog. He didn't bother the hedgehog we had, but then, what does a hedgehog do? You can't cuddle with them, so there was no need for Major to be jealous. Anyway, I still come home and find the pillows on the floor from time to time.

An Obedient Dog

Dogs don't get jealous just of other dogs, though. One time, I was called by a doctor who had just married his fourth wife. Well, he'd bought a German shepherd with his previous wife, and they'd spoiled the dog rotten, even spraying it with Chanel No.5 to make it smell nice, so it had become really used to her. It died before they got divorced, and the doctor didn't realize the spirit of the animal was still around until he married his fourth wife.

It started out that, every day, a picture of the man and his new wife would be knocked off the nightstand by the bed, and no matter what they did, the picture always ended up on the floor. That wasn't a big deal, but then it started to be that, every time they were—shall we say—alone in the bedroom, the burglar alarm would go off. It was set on a motion detector, but after a few times, they came to realize there was no one in the house. They had the alarm company out, and electricians, and nobody could figure out what was wrong—it got to the point where they had to turn off the alarm if they wanted to do anything! He finally broke down and called me.

Sure enough, the spirit of that German shepherd was there, and it did not like the new wife at all. I made the White Light and tried to get it to cross over, but it just wouldn't go, and the man really didn't want it to go, if the truth be known. I knew from my own experiences with Major that a good dog that follows commands will always follow commands, so I had to leave it where he would "take" the dog into a room, when he wanted to be intimate with his wife, and tell it to stay, and even though it could walk through walls if it wanted to, the dog would stay. As far as I know, it worked.

The Dog That Hated Deliverymen

There was another German shepherd I met that held a grudge against certain people. This dog hated—absolutely hated—deliverymen in uniforms, like UPS or the mail carrier or whoever. If they were in a uniform, this dog went crazy—and people knew about it, since it stayed outside most of the time. The family had a fence, but that huge animal would leap up against it and bark ferociously at any delivery person who came near. Clearly, the regular drivers knew about the dog and steered clear.

It eventually died, and the owner started telling the delivery people, when she saw them, that she really would like them to leave packages at the back door, now that the dog was dead. They, of course, understood and took to accommodating her wishes.

Until one day the mail carrier appeared at her front door.

"But I said you could leave packages at the back door!" she said, not understanding why he would want to take the time to ring the bell when he could just drop it and go on about his business.

"I know," the mail carrier replied. "But you got a new dog, you?"

153

"I don't have a dog!" the woman gasped, figuring he was pulling her leg.

"Well, I was heading back there, and I heard its claws clicking on the concrete, and I could hear its tags clinking, and then it began to growl, just like the old one always did."

"But I don't have a dog! The other one died, and I never got a new one!"

With nothing left to say, the mail carrier handed her the package and left.

A few days later, the woman went out back to tidy up the yard a bit, wondering if seeing all of the dog's stuff had unnerved the poor guy, and when she stepped onto the back stoop, she saw the dog's water bowl sitting there.

"I know I put that bowl by his house," she mumbled to herself, recalling uneasily that the only time the bowl had ever moved had been when her dog had put it there to ask for water. As she bent down to pick it back up, she froze; there was the softball-sized rock the dog had always played with, not sitting in the doghouse where she'd put it, but rather right by the bowl, just like when the dog had wanted to play. It was odd, especially with the mail carrier's story, but she didn't think too much of it.

Then the UPS guy showed up at the front door the next day, package in hand.

"Was the gate locked?" she assumed.

"No!" the man almost shrieked. "I thought you said that dog was dead! What kind of joke is that?"

"Joke?" the woman asked. "But he is dead! He died weeks ago!"

"Well, then it must be his brother slinking around back there, because I saw him clear as day."

The comment shook the woman—and she knew for certain that the UPS guy knew what the old dog had looked like.

That was enough for her, so the lady called me. Sure enough, there was a beautiful German shepherd hanging out in the backyard, just as it had always done. I could see it, of course, but she couldn't, and I had to wonder how the UPS man had seen it, as had some of the other delivery people. I asked her if she could remember if there had been a full or new moon the night before or around the sightings, but she couldn't remember.

I'm willing to bet there had been, as that's when a spirit's energy is strongest, yet you also have to remember how afraid those delivery people had been of that dog. Maybe they were so scared and expecting to see it that they put themselves into the right mindset to do just that. But then, even little Major can knock the pillows off a couch, so who knows? Maybe dogs can channel the energy better than humans.

Anyway, I asked her if she wanted to have the dog cross over, and she said she really didn't mind, but that she was moving soon and was afraid it wouldn't follow her—not to mention that she didn't want the animal scaring people, whether it was dead or alive.

So I made the White Light right in the middle of the yard and had the woman hand me this dog's rock. Its face lit up, and it wagged its tail, since nobody had played with it for so long. Then I got the dog beside me and tossed the rock straight into the Light. When it jumped in after it, I closed up the Light, and that was that. The rock didn't actually go in, of course—it was sitting in the middle of the yard, just like I'd tossed it through the empty air—but the dog had, and that was all that mattered.

Wild Animals

I see more animals in the wild, now that I know to look for them. They seem to be in groups, larger than what you'd see with living animals. That's not to say I've seen wolves playing around with deer, but they do definitely appear more social once they're dead.

Once I was asked to visit a primitive campground—one of those areas where a farmer with tons of acres realized that camping was more profitable than crops—and it was full of animal spirits. He'd called me out there because campers kept reporting people dressed as Native Americans wandering around, but there were only two there that I could see, though they kept pretty well hidden, peeking at me from behind trees. I knew they'd been around for a while, because they were dressed in the traditional loin-cloth, like you see in the history books, but they didn't seem to want my help.

All I ended up doing was giving the guy a catalog of the spirits: Deer, fox, elk, birds, and the two Native Americans. None of them were hurting anything, and none seemed to want to cross over, and since I'm not sure I understand the beliefs of the Native American spirits, I just left them all alone. He wanted me to force them to leave, but after talking it over, he came to understand that Hollywood had filled his head with nonsense about Native Americans and the curses on their burial grounds.

White Dogs

There is one other spirit I've heard about but not actually seen that I'd have to count as the ghost of an animal. These are the white dogs that truckers see if they've been on the road too long. I've heard reports of black dogs, too, but never from a trucker who's talked to me. Black dogs wouldn't make much sense, however, since the white dogs appear at night to warn a trucker—or any driver—to slow down or wake up or whatever. Most of the time, when drivers recount these tales, they end with a phrase like, "If I hadn't slowed down for that dog, I would've probably died." I'm not sure whether they are the spirits of once-living animals or not. I wish I knew more about them or came across one myself, but even those who have seen a white dog have only seen it in passing, and they never stop to run after it or see where it goes.

Guardians

Walkers

Truck drivers are the best sources of stories about what I have come to term "Walkers." When I first got calls from truckers, I couldn't figure out how they'd heard about me, because they'd call me from New York or Montana or somewhere, usually just wanting to know if what they'd seen could have been a ghost. Finally, I broke down and asked a guy from New York how he'd gotten my name. Turns out he'd been driving his load through northern Ohio at the same time I was doing a radio show, and suddenly it all made sense.

This particular trucker said he had been driving late at night when he saw a young man walking along the side of the road. Since he had been out in the middle of nowhere, the trucker decided to pull over and see if the guy needed a lift; the young man had graciously accepted the offer and climbed into the cab.

The young man turned out to be a real chatterbox, just talking about anything and everything, and at first the trucker was going to tell him to shut up, but then he realized that the talking was keeping him awake, whereas he'd felt himself nodding off before.

Suddenly, the young man turned to him and said, "I have a bad feeling over this next hill," and something in the way he said it made the trucker slow down. As they crested the hill, he saw a broken down car in the middle of the road; if he'd still been tooling along at 60 mph, he would've slammed right into it. Fortunately, he managed to stop, then turned to the young man to thank him for his foresight...but the cab was empty.

Those are the type of spirits I have come to call Walkers, because they never appear in houses and don't seem to be like normal earthbound entities. The truckers are never scared, because they think they're just picking up regular hitchhikers, but then the hitchhiker will vanish, or in talking to other truckers, they'll find out they've all picked up the same hitchhiker along the same stretch of road and that the person somehow saved them all from having accidents. Apparently, Walkers are psychic, which would instantly set them apart from normal spirits.

One fella said he picked this guy up in the middle of a horrendous downpour—so bad that he almost didn't stop in the first place for fear of skidding, but he felt bad for the guy. The hitchhiker was very appreciative, but then, after they'd been driving for a few minutes, he suddenly said, "Let me out here." The trucker told the guy he was crazy, that they were out in the middle of nowhere, but his ride was adamant, so the trucker pulled over to let him out. No sooner had the hitchhiker opened the cab door than he disappeared— and then the trucker heard a great rushing sound and watched the road in front of him get completely washed away by a flash flood that would've wiped him out, if he hadn't stopped.

Some truckers, having had a Walker experience, will go back and try to find the person again, but they never do, even along the same bit of road where a buddy will say he's seen the same spirit. No trucker I've talked to has ever picked up the same Walker twice.

A few have even said they'll find themselves dozing at the wheel and will kind of open their eyes and see someone sitting in the cab next to them, or else they'll see someone in the rear view mirror, looking at them from the sleeping compartment, and it'll snap them wide awake, then there's no one there when they take a good look. The point is, the spirit's appearance wakes them up and helps them realize they are dangerously close to falling asleep at the wheel.

I've even heard some stories where truckers say the wheel was turned for them—beyond their control—saving them from accidents, all of which says to me that these Walkers are not your average earthbound entities, but rather some class of guardian angel or protective spirit.

Protecting Public Servants

Walker-like spirits also appear to cops and firemen. Sometimes a fireman won't be able to open a door, so he'll move on and later discover that there would have been a horrible back draft that would've killed him had he managed to get the door open. Some have even seen ghosts in burning houses that have told them things like, "Stay out of there. The roof's about to collapse," and sure enough, it does. In cases like that, it's possible that it is the spirit of someone who died in the fire. Being so recently dead, they would certainly have the energy to appear, but that wouldn't necessarily give them any psychic abilities to profess accurate warnings. The firemen know they're ghosts, though, because the Walkers make it clear that they are dead so that the firemen don't try to save them.

Normal spirits—of the once-living—aren't so helpful, which further lends fuel to my theory that Walkers—and even white dogs—are a different class altogether. Your usual earthbound entities are here for a specific reason—to catch a murderer or haunt an insurance adjuster or tell someone where the diamonds are hidden, or simply because they're afraid to cross over—but are not here necessarily to help out. In the course of their other concerns, some spirits will make a lot of noise in a section of the house so that when the occupants go to explore, they catch an intruder or spot the start of a fire or something. But if a spirit was a caring, helpful person in life, I suppose it would continue to be so after death, though not in the same sense as a Walker.

Protecting the Earth?

I have come to the conclusion that certain Native Americans, when they die, are expected to remain earthbound to protect Earth. I have never run across a Native American indoors—they're always outside, apparently guarding some area of land. I suppose it's their heritage, and they've obviously adapted to it, even after death, because I can't imagine where they get their energy. Other spirits need to be around people, which is why they make us feel run-down and sick, but most of the Native Americans I've seen are away from people.

That isn't to say Native Americans are always earthbound simply to watch over Mother Earth and that they adversely affect the living who disturb the land they are watching over. All the Hollywood nonsense about "Indian Burial Grounds"—and cemeteries in general—is just that: nonsense. Anyone can see that, even though their dead appear to be here to protect Earth, they are not actively preventing construction or stopping deforestation. But I assume they remain as some kind of "guardians of Earth," in keeping with their heritage, because I'm not sure what other purpose Native American spirits out in the middle of nowhere could serve—perhaps they are ready to advise any shaman who wanders past? I do know that they don't seem to interfere with the living at all in any negative way.

At least, not intentionally.

I recently went to a reservation out west and got a few answers to some of my questions, raised some more unanswered questions, and settled a few curiosities I had collected. Not only was it the first time I had ever been to a reservation, but as far as I know, it was also the first time a white person had been asked to visit for—shall we say—spiritual business. After all, Native American tribes have a shaman, right? So why on earth would they need the help of a white woman?

Well, what if the last of the tribal shaman had died?

"That's a good question," I said to Laura, the friend of a mutual friend, who knew some Native Americans.

"Yeah, their last shaman died three years ago, and no one wanted to take over. Standing Feather wants you to come out."

"But what for?" I had to ask. It still didn't make sense—wouldn't they at least try to find another tribe's shaman to help them out before they turned to a white woman from Ohio?

"He wants you to take care of an elder who just died. I don't really know, Mary Ann. I just told him what you do, and he asked me to get you out here."

"I've never been out west," I mumbled, thinking aloud. "I won't charge them," I decided, "but I can't afford the plane ticket."

"No problem," Laura replied. "I'll get you out here, and you can stay with me. All you'll have to pay for is your food."

So it was settled. I was really curious about reservations, because I'd never actually been on one, even though I had seen Native American spirits. I wondered if they all stayed behind all the time or if only certain ones remained. Deep down, I hoped I could talk to one, see if anything was different for them. I'd never had any luck talking to them before, let alone getting them into the Light. I'd always written it off as different values and beliefs, even

162

though I'd say we all—no matter what race, creed, or homeland— go into the same Light.

When Laura and I arrived at the entrance to the reservation, we were confronted by a dour Native American who put up a hand for us to stop. He stepped out of his little booth, and I had just began to surmise its purpose when he said, "Five dollars."

"I'm sorry?" I checked.

"Five dollars. You want to go in?"

"Yes."

"Five dollars," he repeated simply, his face not even close to cracking a smile. "Her, too."

I glanced at Laura, who shrugged helplessly. Apparently, this was not the gentleman she had talked to before.

"I'm a guest," I explained. "Standing Feather is expecting me."

The man paused, then finally decided, "Five dollars."

I sighed. Clearly, this was getting nowhere, so I grabbed my purse and dug in it for a bill, while Laura produced her own and handed it to me.

"Here you go," I said with a futile smile. The man took the bills and stuffed them in his shirt pocket, then pointed at the camera on the seat between us.

"You take pictures?"

"Yeah," I said simply, as if it wasn't obvious that a white tourist would want pictures of a reservation.

"Ten dollars," he stated. His face still wouldn't take no for an answer.

"What?" I shrieked. "Look, I'm here to see Standing Feather…"

He didn't care. I sighed and dug in my purse again, producing a 10 dollar bill, which he dutiful took and stuffed in his pocket with the other bills. I knew that other reservations in the area had set up casinos, while this one had pretty much ignored "progress," so I

163

reasoned that they deserved to make their money somehow. Still, he could have been polite, or at least have smiled once.

"Where is Standing Feather?" I asked him as he turned back to his booth. He sort of half-turned at the question and waved in a vague direction, through the gate—but that was all. Laura and I shared a shrug, then moved on before he thought of something else to charge us for.

Inside the reservation it was like a third-world country. There weren't any Hollywood tee-pees and racks of skins and meat or tobacco—just a bunch of shantytown huts and various vehicles held together by rust and wire. Dotted about the landscape were several Native Americans, many with the traditional long hair, but wearing blue jeans and flannel shirts. The younger ones looked mean—they'd have been hoodlums back in Ohio—standing around with cigarettes dangling from their lips and anger in their eyes. I couldn't blame them, exactly, being cooped in a corner of the United States without electricity, running water, or bathrooms. I wanted to tell them to have a little pride and clean themselves up, but then I saw more what was to blame for their run-down, tired condition: In a big open area, just into the center of the reservation, at least 150 Native Americans, U.S. cavalrymen, and Spaniards were doing battle, just as they must have been doing for the last 200 years, sapping all the energy from everyone around them.

That reservation was literally full of ghosts. And hatred—the hatred those spirits must have felt for each other to still be fighting their battle. There was so much negative energy packed into the area that even I began to feel sedentary and tired.

"What?" Laura asked, unconsciously imitating my gaping mouth. I was watching a Native American, knife clenched in his teeth, crawling on his belly toward what was roughly the Spanish area of the battle.

"Hollywood got the fighting all wrong," I finally breathed.

"Huh?" she checked.

"The Indian Wars," I said slowly. "They're still here, fighting. I can see Americans and Indians and Spaniards—and their horses and dogs and everything else—and I can tell you that Hollywood has it all wrong."

I began kind of walking through the fray, and they could see me—the spirits would move out of my way or dodge me, as though I were a walking tree, but they never went through me. I finally reached a Native American and said something so that he'd know I could see him. He turned and looked at me, then went right back to what he was doing. I tried another, but he just ignored me. Finally, I approached a U.S. cavalryman.

"What are you still doing here?" I asked—Laura was sort of tagging along, watching my face for explanations, her eyes wide as if she could somehow catch a glimpse if she tried hard enough.

"Pardon me, ma'am?" he wondered, and I felt relief just to get an answer.

"Why on Earth are you still here?" I repeated. "Aren't you sick of fighting?"

"Yes ma'am," he said without hesitation. "But what else can I do?"

"You realize you're dead, don't you?"

"Yes ma'am," he agreed again and sort of shrugged as though that made his point all the more clear.

"I can make the Light and let you cross over—"

"You can?" he gasped. Without any argument, I made the White Light, and he turned and stepped right in. Another guy caught a glimpse of it, too, and snuck in before I closed it up. So I began to wander around, making the White Light in random locations, and everywhere a handful of the cavalrymen or Spaniards would slink into the Light, not wanting to abandon their post, but not wanting to fight any more, either. They didn't have a sense of the passage of years, as we do, but they could tell from the cars and the clothes on the living that time had passed. One Spaniard, the second I opened the Light, turned and galloped his horse straight in—it was very dramatic, as though he were jumping an invisible fence over into the Light.

But if only a handful of Caucasians took the opportunity to cross over, there were even fewer Native Americans who did so. Even when I made the Light right in the middle of a group of them, they'd just ignore it or walk away. And none of them would so much as nod at me. It wasn't a language barrier, either. I have to believe it was because I am a white woman—but more so because I'm white, since they did have women healers, sometimes. I know it wasn't that they didn't understand me or what the White Light was, because I found out indirectly that, however it is I communicate with spirits, it doesn't require knowledge of their language or for them to speak English.

I had once helped a Hungarian woman's mother cross over, and the daughter had looked at me after a few minutes and asked, "But how are you speaking to my mother?"

"Because, she's standing right here!" I replied.

"But she only speaks Hungarian!" the daughter said. Yet I understood the spirit perfectly, and she understood me. As always, sometimes I have more questions than I do answers.

Anyway, I had watched about 15 spirits cross over—and two horses—and was just beginning to calculate how many weeks it would take me to clear the place out—especially since only 1 in 10 Native Americans would go—when an older-looking, living Native American appeared out of the blue and stepped right up to me.

"Mary Ann?" he assumed.

"Yeah," I said, turning my attention away from the still-raging battle. Every once in a while, they'd all sort of retreat to their own corners, but then they'd just start up again a few minutes later. It's the closest thing I've seen to what I have come to think of as the "European Ghost Phenomenon," in which the ghosts simply replay the same event at the same time, over and over again, like a video player, running down the same hallway in the same way, day after day. Before the reservation, I had never seen such action in America.

"Thank you for coming," the man said. "I am Standing Feather. Follow me."

Apparently small-talk and smiles were not attributes of the tribe—not surprising with all the spirits around—so I hurriedly caught up to him as he walked off across the center of the battle. Laura—a bit shaken from what I'd said, I think—chose to stay behind and kind of hover near the gate, at least for the time being.

"You've got a lot of spirits here," I said, trying to sound friendly.

"Lot of negative energy," he agreed, glancing at me dourly. "There is a lot of negative energy."

"Why won't any of your people talk to me?" I asked him.

He kind of gave me the once over, as if himself realizing for the first time that I was white, then shrugged and let the insinuation stand as explanation.

"Well, why do they hang around then?" I wondered, trying a different angle. "I've run across them before, out in the middle of nowhere…"

Instead of answering, he stopped in front of an adobe-like shanty and pulled back the rug that was a door, indicating that I should go in. I stepped into the dark hovel—it measured maybe 20 feet by 20 feet, with four tiny, six-inch window holes—and before my eyes adjusted to darkness, I noticed the most rotten smell I have ever come across in my life. It was a deep funk, and I knew it wasn't simply that they used one corner as a toilet—I knew what the smell was, and as my eyes adjusted more and more, I began to see the outline of a body on the bed.

"You didn't," I gasped, covering my nose and mouth.

"What?" Standing Feather asked, stepping aside to let me pass back through the doorway.

"Is that his body?" I checked once we were back outside.

"We saved it," he agreed. "So you could lay your hands on it."

"I'm not bringing him back to life!" I said plainly. "His spirit doesn't need his body! When did he die?"

"Three weeks ago."

Three weeks that poor man's body had been lying in his bed, completely unembalmed, and not even drained of blood! Sure, it got to 30 or 40 degrees at night, but by nine o' clock that morning it was already 80 degrees!

"That was really unnecessary."

He stood for a second, waiting for me to say or do something else, and the first thing that came to mind was, "You know, they charged us to get in here?"

"Hmm," he shrugged, uninterested.

"Where is your shaman?" I tried.

"Shaman's dead."

"Why bring me here then? Isn't there someone else who can perform the rituals?"

"No one to take his place. No medicine men—no one wants to do it. Wait here. You'll go with us when we take care of the body." Then he turned to walk off.

"I'll go wait with Laura," I replied, pointing at her. Standing Feather nodded, then strode over to the other end of the row of shanties. I ambled back to Laura, mystified so far by everything that had happened. Sometimes, this life of mine amazes me.

"Well?" she asked.

"They have the body in there!"

"No!" she gasped.

"Yeah," I sighed. "He went off to do something. I'm supposed to go with them to bury it."

"What do you mean?" Laura wondered, narrowing her eyes. "Go with them?"

"Yeah, that's what Standing Feather said. He wants me to go with them when they bury—what's wrong?"

"You must have misheard him," she said with finality, shaking her head. "They don't take white people to their burial grounds."

"That's what he said!"

"No, he couldn't have. And a woman, too? No—he must've said something else."

Suddenly, three or four pick-ups came out of nowhere and revved up to us in clouds of dust and rust. Standing Feather hopped out of one, which I could see had the elder's body in the back, and came over to me.

"We go now. Come."

He began to walk back around to the driver's side, but when I said. "Let's go, Laura," he stopped and spun back to us, his long hair whipping dramatically around him.

"NO! She stays, you go."

I glanced at Laura; she shrugged helplessly.

"Will you have to kill me once I know where you bury him?" I joked nervously, but Standing Feather apparently saw no humor in the comment.

"You'll come back."

And then he was in the truck, starting the engine, so I had no choice but to hop in next to him.

He led the procession up the mountain, and I have no idea how

169

they managed to create a road—which was really just a swath of dirt full of rivulets and potholes—that sloped off to a sheer drop on either side. As we jostled and bounced along, I began to think I wouldn't make it up the mountain alive, let alone back down, so I kept my eyes on the floor, convinced that, any second, we'd go off the edge, and I'd die in a ditch, out in the middle of nowhere, and Ted just wouldn't hear from me again.

Then the engine slowed, the truck stopped jostling so much, and I looked up onto the most beautiful meadow, surrounded by trees, still with some snow in the shady corners. Here and there, markers were dotted, and where people hadn't been buried underground, they were covered with piles of rocks.

We had reached the burial grounds.

Standing Feather and the others went straight to work. They'd wrapped the body in a cloth, and three of them took it from the truck and placed it right on top of a funeral pyre, tossing a few sticks over it for good measure. I kind of backed away, unsure what, exactly, I was supposed to do. Some of them started the flames kindling, and then they all disappeared into a little adobe building off to one side.

As I waited, I tried to converse with the elder's spirit, but he said nothing and didn't even seem to notice that I was there—or wasn't bothered by my presence one way or the other. Finally, the group of men returned, all decked out in feathers and face paint. Some of them carried drums, and they circled around the pyre and began to beat the drums and chant, dancing around the flames much as they have done for hundreds of years. I was fascinated by it, and I backed up to a large flat rock—not a grave—and sat down, wondering why I was there. Why me? Why was I allowed to witness this ritual? And what was my purpose to be?

After about 15 minutes, the meadow suddenly became very quiet. My eyes had wandered—searching for rattlesnakes and scorpions to avoid—so I looked back over to them, and they were all standing motionless, staring up into the sky. I followed their gaze and saw the most gorgeous bird I have ever seen, circling over the pyre. The sun glinted off its feathers like golden glitter, and I realized as it swooped and glided that it was an eagle—a great, gorgeous eagle, soaring over the pyre without a sound. Just this massive, majestic bird that glistened against the blue sky like a golden comet.

I thought of taking its picture, but they had told me I wasn't allowed to take pictures at the burial ground, so I just sat and gazed up at the bird, like them, transfixed, thinking how it must be true, that eagles really do come down to guide their spirits across to the Other Side. Suddenly, the eagle did three really close fly-bys, then swooped back and disappeared over the top of the mountain. When I looked back down at the men, Standing Feather was heading straight for me, his face still dour, and all of the other men were likewise silently glaring at me.

The first thing I assumed was that I had somehow frightened the bird off, so I stood quickly to apologize, though I couldn't imagine what I had done.

Standing Feather stopped right in front of me and announced. "You brought the eagle."

"What? No I didn't..." I realized he didn't mean I'd kept it in my purse and then released it at the right moment—he meant that I, in some sacred fashion, had brought the eagle to them.

"You brought the eagle," he said again. But this wasn't like the man wanting five dollars, and I wasn't going to give up so easily.

"No, I did not. I was just sitting here—I wasn't even paying attention!"

He nodded once. "Thank you. You brought the eagle."

"Doesn't the eagle always come?" I wondered, trying not to offend him. "I mean, isn't that how your spirits are guided across...?"

171

"Not always," Standing Feather said, his eyes fixed on mine. There was no malice, just strong conviction. "Sometimes a bald eagle will come, but not always. That was a golden eagle," he pointed out. "In my whole life, I have never seen a golden eagle come here. You brought the eagle. It is an omen for us and will bring us good luck. I am glad we brought you out here."

I was floored by the whole thing—from the ghostly battle still raging down the mountain to the appearance of a rare golden eagle. The thing was, when I looked over, I saw that both the elder's spirit and his Light were still there—and we left them there, too. I knew that his Light would stay with him for another few days, but I still hadn't seen him cross over or been able to make him go into it, and Standing Feather never even asked about the dead man and never asked me to make sure he crossed over. To this day, I have no idea what purpose I was supposed to serve up there. If the eagle hadn't shown up, would they have asked me to do something? All I can tell you is what I observed, and it seemed to me that they had simply wanted me there, even if I wasn't to do anything. The eagle was really just a fortuitous occurrence—but I learned that the bird hadn't come for the elder's spirit after all. I had sort of expected to see the ghost climb onto its back and ride off, but nothing happened, so maybe it had just been an omen of good luck.

As we proceeded back down the mountain, I realized that I was not going to convince Standing Feather—or the others—of anything other than I had been responsible for the eagle's appearance. Their attitude did soften toward me, because they were vehement that I had a lot of sacred power, but still, none of them seemed concerned about what had become of their elder.

"So, what else can I do, now that you've got me out here?" I asked once we'd reached the bottom of the mountain. Standing Feather was leading me back to his hut, and Laura had caught up to us to try and learn what happened by listening in, until we could talk more privately.

Standing Feather stopped and looked at me curiously, further proving that he hadn't expected me to do anything other than show up.

"I can get rid of some of these spirits," I said, glancing at some of the more modern ghosts still hanging around, but not sure what I could do—given the limited time I had—about the age-old battle still raging.

"Whatever you can do, do," he said, so I kind of wandered off, making the White Light and letting spirits cross over, at the same time filling Laura in on what had happened.

When I'd done all I felt I could do, Standing Feather nodding sagely at my report, but didn't seem too concerned. Apparently I had already done enough for him, because he produced a pair of cougar-paw earrings fashioned out of silver and handed them to me.

"Thank you for coming," he said sincerely.

But I never did get my entrance fee back.

Afterword

On June 7, 1998, during the writing of this book, Grandma Maria passed away. It was a difficult time for me, not only because of my fondness for her, but also because now, after so many years of talking to the spirits of other people's deceased loved ones, I was left having to talk to one of my own. And she was upset.

Grandma had been left partially paralyzed—a perfectly sound mind trapped in a body that had given out. Subsequently, for the last 12 years of her life, she had been in a nursing home—a move for which she never forgave her remaining children. As she sat there on top of her casket, watching the proceedings, she just kept saying again and again how good it felt to be free from her paralyzed body—and out of the nursing home. Then she'd get upset again about having been in the home to begin with, and besides that, she was upset at the funeral home, because they hadn't done her up with lipstick and nail polish, nor her jewelry.

"Mary Ann, just look at me!" she said with dismay. She'd already been griping my ear off about the nursing home, and it wasn't even like the home had been so horrible. She'd been in one of those fancy, private homes—but I still knew how she must have felt. From having visited her, I could see that the home lacked the quality of life she had been accustomed to, and once she died, I felt nothing but relief for her. Not relief in the sense that I was glad to see her go, but relief for her, because that part of her life was now over.

"What now, Nona?" I sighed.

"I look horrible! No lipstick—and where's my nail polish? You know I'd never be caught dead without nail polish."

I smirked dryly at her choice of phrase. "That's not funny, Nona."

"Well," she huffed. "Look at me!"

"Fine," I decided, digging into my purse. I produced a bottle of nail polish and a tube of lipstick, which I held up for her to see. She furrowed her brow slightly and watched with a certain detached amazement as I leaned over and stuffed them into the casket beside her.

"There," I stated, putting my hands on my hips. "Is that better?"

She chuckled amiably, more as I always remembered her to be. None of my family asked what I was doing, but then I imagine there were a lot of other trinkets hidden in the casket with Grandma Maria. She had been very respected throughout the whole family, and I do know that someone had put some bobby pins in there with her, the kind with a rhinestone at the end that she had liked so much. Besides which, I had stated loudly enough for the family to hear—when I was accosted the moment I walked in the door—that I was not at work; that I was there to pay my respects and was not going to play any question-and-answer games with Grandma Maria. Thankfully, they respected that, even though they must have been burning with curiosity to find out what we were talking about.

"Thank you," she winked as I straightened back up, then her face dropped again. "I know what you're doing, Mary Ann."

"What?"

"I have more loose ends than lipstick and nail polish to tie up before I go into that Light."

I just gaped, then finally managed to say what I was thinking.

"After all these years, Grandma—after all those people you dragged me along to make sure they crossed over—and now you're saying you're not going?"

"That's right. I have a score to settle."

"What score?" I begged. "Grandma, you really have to cross over, you know that. And you know you can still come back."

"Don't talk down to me, Mary Ann!" she jabbed back. "I know what I can and can't do, and I know you can't force me across. I also know I can't get even once I've crossed over."

"Get even?" I gasped. "What are you talking about?"

"My loving kids who stuffed me in that nursing home. I'm going to fix them."

"Fix...?" I sighed and put my hands on my hips. "Come on, Nona, you know they did what they thought best."

"No. They deserve it."

"Nona, you have to cross over."

"No I don't," she stated defiantly. "And you can't make me." Aside from the vengeance aspect, I think Grandma Maria was staging a sort of protest for me. All her life, I had let her believe—out of respect—that she was my teacher and I the student, even though from very early on I knew that my abilities were considerably more vast than hers. Certainly she was more knowledgeable in areas about life and the wisdom of having lived, but when it came to our special abilities, I was more advanced—though I would never have told her that—and as soon as she died, it became obvious, and she didn't like that one bit.

"So that's what this is about," I said thoughtfully. She not only wanted to get back at her kids for the nursing home ordeal, but now she wanted to satiate some kind of inferiority complex about our abilities. She was right, though: I couldn't force her to cross over any more than I could force anyone to cross over. Especially someone I knew so well—and knew to be hard-headed, when the mood took her.

176

"Fine," I said, not trying to hide my anger at her. "You can stay—that's your choice—but you will not bother your family." I dug in my purse again and produced a handful of the quince seeds I use to protect a home from spirits. She knew what they meant: I use them on every home I work on and even give them to people—like cops or nurses, who are forever in danger of ghosts attaching themselves to them—to carry around at all times. I don't know how they work, but the tiny seeds form some sort of barrier that spirits cannot cross or get near. If a spirit does try, the seed will pop, but it still won't be able to haunt the protected home or person. You'd be amazed how many seeds cops go through. Even though I tell them popped seeds work just as well as whole seeds, they still want to trade them in for fresh ones, which means I basically run my own import business on Italian quince seeds. (I get them from people—distant relatives—in Grandma Maria's old village, who "make" them especially for me. What they do to them, or why quince seeds, I don't know—I just know they work!)

"I will put these seeds over every inch of their homes if I have to," I warned her. Normally they just go over doorways, because spirits, even though they can walk through walls, still always use the doors. Sometimes I'll put them over windows, too, in extreme cases.

"You can stay," I concluded, "but you won't bother them."

It was like an international chess match for her, you could just tell. She was sitting there, trying to fathom an answer, and she finally came up with, "What if I go now, Mary Ann? Before you get there?" She smirked triumphantly.

"Which one?" I asked. "Who are you going to haunt? You can't be in three places at once, and you know I'm protected, so it's no good hanging on to me. Besides, if you leave now, you'll never see who came to your funeral or hear what they have to say." And our family funerals are pretty raucous events that I can't imagine any spirit wanting to miss. Instead of sitting quietly and crying, we are loud—very loud—laughing and reminiscing like it were a reunion, not a funeral.

Grandma knew she wanted to be there and didn't know how to reply, so she just huffed, "Well, I'm still not going. You can't make me." A real queen bee, right to end.

It's ironic—like the cobbler whose children go barefoot. Here I am, in such demand to get rid of ghosts that it has become my job, but I was unable to get the very woman who had once told me that if I told a spirit to go, it had to go, to cross over herself! Her surviving children know she was upset at them—I didn't have to be very diplomatic in what I revealed to my own family, after all—and they also know that she refused to cross over. But either the seeds worked, or she snuck across once we'd all left, because I haven't seen her since the funeral, nor have I even dreamed of her. Maybe she just wanted to tour the world a bit, after years of being paralyzed. Maybe she just needed time to adjust, as I think we all do.

I think we could help out spirits by returning to longer funerals, so they have a longer period in which to cross over. The way it is now, you die today, are shown tomorrow, and buried the next day, then before you know it, with the ritual over, the Light has gone away, and if you didn't cross over, you're stuck, and at some point all spirits—even those overjoyed with their new understanding of immortality—get bored. Or else they see the passage of time—not days and weeks like us, but they see the changes around them, in cars and fashions—and it scares them or frustrates them, and they begin to make nuisances of themselves. At least I know Grandma Maria's aware of how to cross over by herself when she's ready.

In a way, Grandma Maria exemplifies all I've come to believe about death, and even birth: It's all free will. We can cross over when we die if we want, or we can choose to stay. The same is true for coming back—being reincarnated. Some people never seem to understand that. Crossing over is not The End. We can come back once we've crossed over, either as a spirit that can't interfere with the living or reborn to do it all over again. I believe the other side of the White Light is a heaven-like place, but maybe more of a learning experience than anything. It's like a spiritual ladder we have to climb, and the bad people start at a lower rung. We can just stay over there if we want, but I believe it's a faster climb up the rungs if we come back into corporeal form and live another life, either to learn something ourselves or to teach someone else something.

But that's all speculation. I honestly don't know what is on the Other Side—just what makes sense after years of dealing with things like this. There are people who can see spirits that have crossed over—there are some that can only see spirits that have crossed over—but my own unique ability is earthbound spirits, and I don't think God wants me to know—or needs me to know—any more. I asked one spirit at a funeral, who was talking to her relatives in the Light, to ask them what they were seeing over there. Could they see God? Angels? What was it like? But they wouldn't tell her, just like no spirit has ever told me where they get their clothes or cigarettes. It might not be that they won't tell the earthbound—live or dead—so much as they can't. Maybe we can't understand the Other Side until we've experienced it. Whatever it is, I do know that it's Good, and that we have to cross over—ironically, that's a part of life.

Some spirits just don't believe me, though—some of them don't even believe I can talk to them! One lady was convinced I was a witch. I'm not a witch, as I told her—I'm a Catholic. I believe very deeply in God and am still a regular churchgoer. After all, He is the one who blessed me with this ability to help Him get people into the Light. Not to say I am "chosen" in some way: These abilities are born naturally into each and every one of us; I was just lucky enough to have Grandma Maria there to nurture them.

I think most people, if they really wanted to, even after having it "bred" out of them, could regain the same abilities. All the people whose houses I do, once the ghost is gone, have something to base their "feelings" on and can recognize what the spirit "felt" like, and can then recognize it when they go to other places that are haunted. But I can't teach it to people, since I'm not really sure how I do it. I have just always done it, so there was never a learning process for me to pass on to others.

At times, I have felt a more specific Divine Guidance, like when I developed the ability to sense ghostly energies over the phone. That was a direct gift from God, in response to a prayer. He knew He had to make it easier for me, and He did so in a very convenient way! Other times, I've found answers to my most troubling questions just by thinking about the question before I go to bed. When I wake up in the morning, I usually have the answer, whether from God or a guardian angel I can't say, but it's there nonetheless.

In many ways, I've been very fortunate in my relationship with God and the things I've learned. I don't really think about death, just spirits. It'd be a wonderful world if everyone who died crossed over, but they don't, and I think about them, but I've never been afraid to die because of it—even when I was a little girl. When I had kids, I didn't want to die, but that's just because I wanted them to be raised correctly! I remember asking God, when each of my newborns was placed in my arms, to let me live at least long enough to see them grow up. And when the girls were about 13 and 16, I was watching them playing by the pool, and I thought, "Well, God, thank you." It was just a sudden realization of, Hey, thanks, they're grown up now.

People are afraid of dying mostly because they think it will hurt. I'm sure I have a greater sense of peace about it because I've seen what happens when we die—and I know it doesn't hurt—but I can't seem to get that sense across to others. Yes, I'm sure a murder victim experiences pain to the body, but not from the actual dying. As soon as you die, all the bodily pain goes away—there is no feeling of being severed or cut off from the body. From the world and loved ones, yes, but that's an emotional pain; dying doesn't hurt in a physical way.

And I truly believe no one dies before his or her time.

With my belief in reincarnation, I'm not so sure that everyone doesn't know, from day one, exactly when and how they will die. It is our choice to be reborn—or born at all—and we decide what to teach ourselves in that life, and what to teach others. God doesn't force us to be reborn, and He doesn't force us to die—we decide all of that, and He accepts it. It's our choice; we have complete free will. Even with the darkest, most negative energies I've run across, I can't help but imagine they could cross over into the Light, too—God is all-forgiving, after all. The comforting thing is that "demons" couldn't be reborn from the Light if they crossed over. They can only be called back from whatever negative place it is they normally reside in, and only then with the help of a living person, who would have to compromise his or her soul.

People have asked, with all I seem to know and what I surmise from it, if I've ever tried to cross into the White Light myself, just to see what's over there and answer my own questions. Well, I haven't. I'm not even sure if I could make it and walk into it, to be honest—or whether I would just end up banging into a wall or simply end up on the other side of the room, like the dog's rock I threw "into" the Light to get him to cross over. But at the same time, I don't need to go into the Light while I'm alive. For one thing, if God wanted me to know what was over there, He'd tell me or show me in some other way.

One thing I do know is that, when I die, I'll have plenty of time to explore the Other Side because I'm going straight in and I'm tak-

181

ing a long vacation! I just need to sit over there and watch; get some more answers.

As we all do, perhaps.

Over the years, I have come to realize that I can't possibly get everyone over there, no matter what. So I close all my lectures—and now this book—with a quick lesson on how to cross over, should you find yourself stuck. Every time I say that, I can see the eyes of the people listening to me perk up—I'm offering them a chance to stick around as an immortal, but with a way out when they get bored! I never used to tell people, assuming they would just cross over if I impressed it upon them enough, but now I see that may not be the case. It's that whole choice thing again. Besides, one day I will die, and people need to know what to do when I'm not there to tell them!

Quite simply, every White Light is a Universal Light: Anyone can use any Light to cross over. If you get stuck, find a funeral home or even a life-support patient and sneak into the Light of whoever is there—they're not going to mind.

Regardless, I hope you have learned one thing from this book: Once you're dead, it's not fun here anymore. This is the physical world, and it's no place for spirits. Tie up your loose ends—if you can—and move on. We must cross over into the spirit world to learn—it's a part of life.

And don't forget: Once you've crossed over, you can always come back, one way or another.

About the Authors

Mary Ann Winkowski was born in Cleveland, Ohio, with the ability to see and talk to Earthbound spirits. She has since used her abilities to help countless people around the world affected by Earthbound spirits or negative energy. She also inspired and served as a consultant on the CBS television show *Ghost Whisperer* and is the author of *When Ghosts Speak*; *Beyond Delicious: The Ghost Whisperer's Cookbook*; and two works of fiction based on her experiences, *The Book of Illumination* and *The Ice Cradle*. Mary Ann still lives in Cleveland with her husband, Ted, and Just Fred, their red-and-white cat. She also has two grown daughters. Visit Mary Ann online at **maryannwinkowski.com**.

David Powers earned a degree in Creative Writing from Ohio University. He has worked as a freelance music critic, a section editor at an alternative newsweekly, and is currently a technical writer, creating help files for a leading software developer. His fiction has appeared under the name David Christopher in magazines such as *Lost Worlds*, *The MacGuffin*, and England's *Enigmatic Tales*. He recently launched "OH Hellmouth," a fiction blog inspired by "weird" Ohio at **graveworm.com**.

Made in the USA
Lexington, KY
25 November 2011